D0153995

Oracle **Database Administration**

Interview Questions
You'll Most Likely Be Asked

357
Interview Questions

VIBRANT
PUBLISHERS

Oracle **Database Administration**
Interview Questions
You'll Most Likely Be Asked

ISBN-10: 1-946383-00-7
ISBN-13: 978-1-946383-00-6

Library of Congress Control Number: 2014917511

This publication is designed to provide accurate and authoritative information in regard to the subject matter covered. The author has made every effort in the preparation of this book to ensure the accuracy of the information. However, information in this book is sold without warranty either expressed or implied. The Author or the Publisher will not be liable for any damages caused or alleged to be caused either directly or indirectly by this book.

Vibrant Publishers books are available at special quantity discount for sales promotions, or for use in corporate training programs. For more information please write to **bulkorders@vibrantpublishers.com**

Please email feedback / corrections (technical, grammatical or spelling) to **spellerrors@vibrantpublishers.com**

To access the complete catalogue of Vibrant Publishers, visit
www.vibrantpublishers.com

Table of Contents

Oracle Database Administration Interview Questions

Review these typical interview questions and think about how you would answer them. Read the answers listed; you will find best possible answers along with strategies and suggestions.

This page is intentionally left blank.

Chapter 1

Basic Administration

1: You as a DBA just gathered the statistics on schema A. Schema A has 1500 tables. You want to know the name of the table with the highest number of records without running a count on each. How do you do this?

Answer:

You query the NUM_ROWS column in the DBA_TABLES table. After running the statistics, this field is populated with current and updated data, and it is simple and quick method for getting this information without going to every table and counting the records.

2: List four possible ways (direct or indirect) to execute an SQL query against an Oracle Database.

Answer:

a) **Using the SQL*Plus command line tool**. With this tool, you can directly execute SQL commands.

b) **Using a GUI (Graphical User Interface) tool** like SQL Developer. You can directly execute SQL commands with such tools.

c) **Using Oracle Enterprise Manager**. This is an indirect way of executing an SQL query. When you perform certain operations with Oracle Enterprise Manager, they are converted to SQL queries implicitly and these SQL queries are executed against the database.

d) **Writing your own program**. This is not a conventional way of executing your queries but actually it is widely used. Any web or windows program that uses Oracle database at backend, executes SQL queries. These programs are written using a programming language like .NET or JAVA and they use a driver to connect to database.

3: What is SQL*Plus? How can one acquire it and what kind of operations can be performed with it?

Answer:

a) SQL*Plus is a command line tool developed by Oracle Corporation.

b) It is freely distributed. It is shipped with Oracle client installations or Oracle database installations as a default. So, if Oracle client or Oracle database software is installed on a computer, you can find it under "$ORACLE_HOME/bin/" directory. The name of the executable is "sqlplus" on Linux systems and "sqlplus.exe" on Microsoft Window Systems.

c) You can connect to an Oracle database with it. Once connected, you can execute Oracle commands or SQL queries against the connected database. SQL*Plus has also its own commands for formatting the output so that you can display the results in a neat way.

4: A user is logged on to a Linux server as root where Oracle database is running. The Oracle is installed at "/u01/app/oracle/product/11.2.0.4/dbhome" and the name of the SID is "ORCL". The user wants to connect to the database locally using operating system authentication with SYSDBA privileges. Show the command that the user has to execute.
Answer:

a) First he needs to switch to "oracle" user:

su - oracle

b) Later he needs to set required environment variables:

$ export ORACLE_SID=ORCL

$ export ORACLE_HOME=/u01/app/oracle/product/11.2.0.4/dbhome

c) Finally he needs to execute the following command to connect to database:

$ /u01/app/oracle/product/11.2.0.4/dbhome/bin/sqlplus / as sysdba

5: In our organization, we're using an Oracle database whose version is 11.2.0.4. Explain what each digit shows.

Answer:

"11": This first digit shows the major database version. Oracle usually publishes a major release once a 4 year. This digit is usually followed by a character describing the nature of the release. For example: 9i (internet), 10g (grid), 11g (grid), 12c (cloud).

"2": This second digit shows the maintenance release number of the software. Oracle publishes the major release as maintenance release 1 and then usually publishes a second maintenance release during the life time of the software. New features are added to database software with maintenance releases.

"0": This third digit is Fusion Middleware Number. This will be 0 for database software.

"4": This fourth digit is called Component-Specific Release Number and it shows the path set update that was applied to the software. Patch set updates are published 4 times a year by Oracle and as you apply them to your database software, this fourth digit advances.

6: You're at a client's office and you are expected to solve a problem in their database. The client is not sure about their database version and you want to find out the version of their existing database. Describe three different methods you can use to find the version of database software.

Answer:

a) You can find the version by connecting to the database with SQL*Plus. SQL*Plus will print the name and the version of the database software once you're connected to the database. A sample output will look like below:

"Connected to:

Oracle Database 11g Enterprise Edition Release 11.2.0.4.0 - Production

With the Partitioning, OLAP, Data Mining and Real Application Testing options"

b) You can find the version by querying the "v$version" view. You can execute the SQL query below to find the version of the database:

SQL> SELECT * FROM v$version;

A sample output would look like below:

BANNER

Oracle Database 11g Enterprise Edition Release 11.2.0.4.0 - Production

PL/SQL Release 11.2.0.4.0 - Production

CORE   11.2.0.4.0   Production

TNS for Linux: Version 11.2.0.4.0 - Production

NLSRTL Version 11.2.0.4.0 - Production

c) You can find the version from Enterprise Manager. If you logon to Oracle Enterprise Manager, the version of the database software will be listed at the home page under "General" web part.

7: Your client said that he forgot the password for "SYSTEM" user of his database and he no longer could connect. How would you recover this admin password?

Answer:

a) If there are other users who have "DBA" privileges, you can connect with those users and change the password for "SYSTEM" user. The users who have DBA privileges have the privileges to change any user's password. This option is the easiest method but this may not be the case in all scenarios.

b) If there are no other users with "DBA" privileges then the only way to connect to the database is to connect using operating system privileges. The oracle software runs under a specific user at operating system. This user is usually named "oracle". Also, there needs to be a user group that "oracle" user belongs. This user group is usually named "dba". The operating system users who belong to "dba" group can connect to database with "SYSDBA" privileges. So, you need to ask the system administrator to logon to server as "oracle" user or any user who belongs to this "dba" group. Once logged on to operating system, you can connect to database locally using operating system authentication with SYSDBA privileges. After connecting to the database, you can change the reset the password for this system user.

8: What is a password file and why is it needed?

Answer:

Passwords for database users are stored in the data dictionary of the database. When a user wants to login to the database, the username and password provided by the user is checked against the values stored in the database. If the username and password match, the user is granted access to database. The data dictionary is part of the database and it will be accessible as long as the database is open. The passwords for administrators are stored in the dictionary as well.

When the database is closed, the data dictionary will be inaccessible. There needs to be a mechanism for administrators to logon to database even when it is closed, because it is one of the administrator's tasks to start up a down database. A password file is a separate operating system file that is stored on disk outside of the database. The username and password for the users who have SYSDBA or SYSOPER privileges are stored in it. Administrators who have those privileges are authenticated using this password file even when the database is down.

9: You want to find out how many users are defined in the password file and what privileges those user have. How would you accomplish this?

Answer:

You need to query the "v$pwfile_users" view to get information about the existing users in the password file.

Execute the SQL query below:

sql> SELECT * FROM v$pwfile_users;

The query above will return four columns for each user in the password file. The column names are USERNAME, SYSDBA, SYSOPER and SYSASM.

a) The USERNAME column shows the username of the user in the password file.

b) The SYSDBA column shows whether the user has SYSDBA privileges or not.

c) The SYSOPER column shows whether the user has SYSOPER privileges or not.

d) The SYSASM column shows whether the user has SYSASM privileges or not.

10: What would be the main responsibilities of an Oracle DBA in an organization?

Answer:

a) The main duty of an Oracle DBA is to keep the Oracle Databases of the organization up and running. This may involve installing and configuring a database from scratch.

b) On a running system, the DBA will be the only privileged person who can shut down and start up the database.

c) The DBA will create new users and manage the privileges of each user.

d) He will take regular backups to ensure that data is safe.
    In case of a disaster, he will be responsible of restoring
    the database from backups.

e) He will have to do monitor the space usage and do
    capacity planning for the database. He will be
    responsible for enforcing security policies. He will have
    to monitor database activities.

f) He will have to tune the database so that it works at an
    acceptable speed.

g) He is expected to follow the latest patches and apply
    them when applicable.

**11: How does an Oracle DBA role differ from an Oracle
Developer role in an organization? Are there any similarities
between these too?**

Answer:

An Oracle developer is mainly responsible for developing
backend applications. They do data modelling according to
business rules. They design tables, create indexes and other
type of constraints. They are expected to know SQL and
PL/SQL. The develop procedures using this languages.
However, the Oracle developers are not expected to administer
the database software itself.

On the other side, an Oracle DBA's main duty is to administer
the database which involves tasks like doing maintenance to
keep the databases up and running, taking backups, enforcing
security policies etc. DBAs are not primarily assigned to

develop code. DBAs are supposed to have a good knowledge of SQL and PL/SQL like a developer as these are also required for administering the database.

According to the structure of the organization, DBAs might also be assigned development tasks or at least assist the developers where necessary.

Chapter 2

Creating and Configuring an Oracle Database

12: How do you choose the DB character set, and how is it changed after the database is created?

Answer:

When you choose a character set that will define how all the characters (data and metadata) are stored in the database. This is based on the number of supported client languages. Normally this is a configuration that will not be changed in the future. If however, for some reason, in the future as a consequence of globalization (for example) more character sets need to be supported, you can use a full export/import or use the CSALTER script.

13: There are 10 identical servers and you want to install Oracle Database on each of them. What would you use to automate the installation process?

Answer:

If you are going to do batch installations, it is best to do it with Oracle Universal Installer in silent mode. For single installations, it is best to start installer in "interactive mode" and set installation options at each window. However in batch installations, this will take long. You need to do the installations in "silent" mode with a "response file". In silent installation, you start the Oracle Universal Installer from a command prompt and specify the location of the "response file".

The installation files and the response file can be shared among the servers via NFS so that you won't have to copy the setup files to each server.

14: You want to create a response file to speed up the installation of databases. How would you prepare a response file?

Answer:

A response file is a plain text file, where options to create a database are stored. It is possible to create it manually from scratch but that would take long and would be erroneous. Installation media comes with a template response file. It is rather easier to customize it manually. This file also contains notes about the parameters.

However the easiest and most reliable way to create a response file is using Oracle Universal Installer. If you start the installer in "record" mode, every option you choose at each step is automatically recorded in a response file in correct format. After the installer completes in "record" mode, you'll have a complete response file with all the options set in it.

15: When creating a database with SQL script, what would you specify in the script?

Answer:

It is also possible to create a database via an SQL script. In this script I would specify:

a) Name of the database

b) Password of the SYS user

c) Password of the SYSTEM user

d) At least three online redolog groups. I would also specify at least two members for each redo log group.

e) Character set and the national character set of the database.

f) Location and size of the SYSTEM and SYSAUX tablespace. These table spaces will be used for holding system data.

g) I would specify a normal tablespace to use as the default tablespace of the database.

h) I would specify a temporary tablespace to use as the default temporary tablespace of the database.

i) I would specify an undo tablespace.

16: What makes up an Oracle Instance?

Answer:

An instance is made up of a shared memory region on RAM called System Global Area (SGA) and background processes. The system global area is a shared memory, which means it can be accessed by multiple processes. This are holds data which is required by the instance to operate.

The background processes are operating system processes and each process has a specific responsibility in the instance.

The System Global Area and background processes are created when the instance is "started". When the instance is "shut down", the processes are killed and the shared memory region is "released" back to operating system.

17: What constitutes an Oracle Database?

Answer:

An Oracle database resides on disk and thus is permanent. It is composed of files that are stored on disk. These files can be categorized into three types:

a) **Data Files**: These files hold "user" data or "system" data. Any data that belongs to an application is an example of "user" data. The "data dictionary" of the database is an example of "system" data.

b) **Online Redo Log Files**: These files hold the "change" records. Any change, which will be made to a data file, is first written to online redo log files.

c) **Control Files**: These files are relatively small but they are essential for a database. They hold information about the physical structure of the database like location of data files, online redo log files etc.

This page is intentionally left blank.

Chapter 3

Database States and Database Operations

18: You are informed by monitoring that database PROD2 is down. When you issue startup the database enters mount but fails to proceed to the next stage. What file allows the database to enter mount mode, and where do you expect to be problems to move past that?

Answer:

If the database enters mount stage, that means that it found and read the control file. Since it hasn't been able to open the database (next stage), there are some issues with at least one of the datafiles of all previously online tablespaces.

19: Which tools can you use to start up an Oracle database?

Answer:

You can start up a database with three tools.

  a) **SQL*Plus**: This is the most widely used option. You

first connect to an idle instance with SQL*Plus and then start up the instance with "startup" command.

b) **Oracle Enterprise Manager**: This is another way of starting up a database. You can logon to Oracle Enterprise Manager even if the database is stopped. OEM will detect the status of the down database and will present you "Startup" button. You can start up the database by clicking this button.

c) **RMAN**: This is rather a less used tool for starting up a database but it is possible to startup a database from Recovery Manager command line.

20: During startup of a database, at which order does Oracle software search a parameter file?

Answer:

A parameter file holds instance parameters which govern how an instance operates. In order to startup an instance, Oracle needs to locate this file.

The search order is as below:

<$ORACLE_HOME>/dbs/spfile<SID>.ora - This is an server parameter file and this is the first place that oracle will look for. <SID> is the service identifier of the instance.

<$ORACLE_HOME>/dbs/spfile.ora - If Oracle cannot find the file in the first location, it will search this file. This is again a server parameter file.

<$ORACLE_HOME>/dbs/init<SID>.ora - This is a parameter file and it is plain text. If Oracle cannot find the two file listed above, it will search for this file. This is the last location to search.

21: At what stages does an instance pass while starting up?
Answer:

You can start up a database with the modes below:

a) **NOMOUNT**: This is the first stage. At this mode the instance is started.

b) **MOUNT**: This is the second stage. At this mode, the instance is started and the database is mounted. However, the database is not open so you cannot still access data. However you can perform several maintenance tasks at this stage.

c) **OPEN**: This is the final stage. The database is open and all the data is accessible. The default open mode is "read/write" which means you can read data or write to it. However, it is also possible to open it in "read only" mode where you can only read data but cannot change it.

22: You want to do maintenance on your database but during the maintenance period, you don't want any user to be able to connect to the database. How would you accomplish this?
Answer:

When a database is open, any user with "CREATE SESSION" privilege can make a connection. However it is possible to open the database in "restricted" mode. When a database is open in restricted mode, only users with "RESTRICTED SESSION" privilege can make a connection to the database. By default, only DBAs have "RESTRICTED SESSION" privilege and it should not be granted to regular users.

Opening a database in "restricted" mode is a good way to prevent regular users from accessing the database during maintenance.

23: Your database is open. You don't want to interrupt currently connected users but you want to temporarily disable further logons. What would you do to achieve this and how would you revert the database back to normal state after that?

Answer:

I would put the database in "restricted mode". While in restricted mode, only users with "RESTRICTED SESSION" privilege can make a connection. I would run the below command to put database in restricted mode:

sql> alter system enable restricted session;

After executing this command regular users won't be able to logon to the database. Once I want to revert the database to normal, I execute this command:

sql> alter system disable restricted session;

24: What are the types of shutdown modes of an Oracle database?

Answer:

a) **Normal**: In this mode, no new connections are allowed and the database is closed after all the sessions disconnect themselves.

b) **Immediate**: No new connections are allowed and the existing active transactions are rolled back. Changes made by an active transaction are lost in this option.

c) **Transactional**: No new connections are allowed and Oracle waits until all active transactions are completed.

d) **Abort**: This happens immediately however the database is not shutdown cleanly. Database will have to perform instance recovery next time it is started. This option should not be used in regular activities.

25: The data files of your database reside on a storage system. You want to take a snapshot of the storage so that you can use it backup purposes. You also want to ensure that no data is written to data files while the snapshot is being taken. Is it possible to accomplish this while the database is open?
Answer:

Yes, it is possible to stop all I/O activity while the database is open. Normally, when a database is open, there will be constant I/O to online redo log files or data files. Even if the database is idle, there is no guarantee that database will not write anything to files during snapshot.

However, if you "suspend" the database, Oracle will halt I/O operations to these data files until it is reverted back to normal mode. So, you should "suspend" the database, take the snapshot of the disk and then put the database back in normal mode immediately after that.

26: What kind of information can be given while creating a sequence?
Answer:

a) **Sequence Name**: This is the name of the sequence. It should be unique inside the schema.

b) **Start With**: This is the number that the sequence will start from.

c) **Increment By**: This number shows how much the sequence will increment at each move.

d) **Nocycle**: This determines whether the sequence will start from the beginning once it reaches the end.

e) **Nocache**: This determines how much next sequence number will be cached in SGA. Nocache means no next sequence will be cached.

Chapter 4

Oracle Background Processes

27: Oracle starts many background processes. Which one will cause the instance to crash if it is killed? Which infrastructure event is this similar to?

Answer:

The PMON process. If you kill this process the effect is the same as of a power outage or a shutdown abort command. The instance is terminated and it will require instance recovery from the redo logs or undo tablespace once it is brought back up.

28: You look in the server and find there are 5 processes starting with P and followed by numbers, P000, P001 up to P004. What are these processes?

Answer:

There are slave processes spawned from parallel queries. This means that there are queries running In a total parallelism of 5.

These should not exceed the number of cores in the server.

29: The LOG_ARCHIVE_MAX_PROCESSES parameter controls the maximum number of processes responsible for which task? What are the names of these processes in the OS? How many are spawned at startup?

Answer:

These processes are responsible for writing the archive logs. The processes are named ARCx with x from 0 to LOG_ARCHIVE_MAX_PROCESSES-1. At startup there are spawned LOG_ARCHIVE_MAX_PROCESSES number of processes and they continue during instance lifetime.

30: You want your database to start automatically, after a reboot of the server. How would you do that?

Answer:

In default configuration, Oracle database will not automatically start after the server reboots. You'll have to start it manually after each reboot. You'll usually want it to start automatically. There are two methods to accomplish this:

a) **Using Oracle Restart**: "Oracle Restart" is a feature of Oracle High Availability Service (OHAS). You need to install "Grid Infrastructure" to enable "Oracle Restart" feature. Using "Oracle Restart" is the recommended way.

b) **Using Your Own Script**: It is also possible for you to write your own "bash" script to start the database and place that script in the startup of the operating system.

31: Which components of your database environment can be protected by an "Oracle Restart" configuration?
Answer:

a) **Database Instances and Automatic Storage Management (ASM)**: Database instances and ASM instances will be restarted if they crash somehow.

b) **Oracle NET Listener**: Oracle NET Listener will be started if it crashes and stops listening for incoming connection.

c) **ASM Disk Groups**: Oracle Restart will mount ASM Disk groups if they are dismounted.

d) **Database Services**: Non-default database services will be started by Oracle Restart feature.

e) **Oracle Notification Services (ONS)**: This is another Oracle component that can be protected by Oracle Restart.

32: Explain the difference between "shared server" architecture and "dedicated server" architecture.
Answer:

When a user connects to a database, he sends SQL queries to the database to execute. These SQL queries are executed by a "server process" and the result is returned back to the user. In "dedicated server" architecture, the instance will create one server process for each connected user. That process will be "dedicated" to that user and will only serve that client. However in "shared server" architecture, a single server process will serve multiple clients. In shared server architecture, the total memory consumption will be less. However, certain operations like DBA activities can only be performed in dedicated server.

33: Explain how "shared server" architecture works.
Answer:

In shared server architecture, the clients connect to a "dispatcher" process. This dispatcher is responsible for delivering the SQL requests to the "request queue".

The shared server process monitors the request queue. When they find an incoming request, they execute this SQL query and place the results in the response queue. The request queue and the response queue reside in the system global area.

The dispatcher processes also monitor response queue. When it receives a result, they deliver the result to the relevant client. In this architecture, there will be multiple shared server processes and dispatcher processes.

34: What are the instance parameters that are used for configuring shared server architecture?
Answer:

a) **DISPATCHERS**: A string value which is used to configure dispatchers.

b) **SHARED_SERVERS**: Minimum number of shared

server processes that will be present in the server. Also, this number of shared servers is created during startup.

c) **MAX_SHARED_SERVERS**: This parameter determines the maximum number of shared server processes that can run at the same time.

d) **SHARED_SERVER_SESSIONS**: This parameter specifies the maximum number of sessions that can exist at the same time using shared server connection.

e) **CIRCUITS**: This parameter determines the maximum number of virtual circuits that can exist in the system.

35: Explain how the "Database Writer" process works.

Answer:

There can be multiple database background processes. They are named as "DBWn" at operating system. This process is responsible for writing "dirty" buffers to disk. When a server process wants to update a data block, it reads the block from disk to buffer cache if the block is not already in the cache and then updates the copy in the cache. The modified database block in the buffer cache is called a "dirty" block.

When there is no more room in the buffer cache for new blocks or when a "checkpoint" occurs in the database, the database writer processes writes these dirty buffers to disk.

36: Explain what role "Log Writer" background process plays in an instance.

Answer:

When something will be changed in a database, the change record is first written to the redo log buffer which resides in the System Global Area and then the change is applied to the actual data block in the buffer. Log Writer process is responsible for writing the redo records to the online redo log files that are stored in the disk. The log writer is named "LGWR" in the operating system.

The records in the redo log buffer are written to disk when a commit occurs or when one-third of the buffer is full.

37: What is a checkpoint in an Oracle Database?

Answer:

When a checkpoint occurs, the dirty buffers in the buffer cache are written to disk and control files and the headers of the data files are updated with the System Change Number (SCN). The checkpoint process signals the database writer process to write dirty buffers to disk and it updates the control file and the headers of the data files itself. There will be one checkpoint in the instance and it will be named "CKPT" in the operating system. The checkpoints affect the instance recovery.

38: How does an instance recovery occur in an instance?

Answer:

In a running instance, any change that will be made to data is first written to online redo log files as change records and after that it is applied to the data blocks. The data blocks updated in the buffer cache which resides in the RAM physically. The data on the disk is not updated directly. When a "commit" occurs in a database, all the records in the redo log buffer are written to online redo log buffers and a "commit" record is also written. Oracle guarantees that the commit records are written to disk. However the data blocks are updated in cache and there is no guarantee that they will be written to disk. The instance may crash and terminate unexpectedly before the modified blocks are written to disk and they are lost. In such a situation, the next time you start the instance, Oracle will read the online redo log files and detect the changes which have not been written to disk yet. Oracle will first apply all those missing changes and then open the database. This process is called "instance recovery" and it happens automatically without the need of manual intervention. The recovery is performed by the System Monitor (SMON) process.

39: How does archiving of online redo log files happen in an instance?

Answer:

Redo records are first recorded in the log buffer which resides in System Global Area by server processes. These redo records are then written to the online redo log files on the disk by log writer process. When an online redo log file is filled a "log file switch" occurs and log writer process starts writing to the next online redo log file. If the database is working in "archive log" mode then the filled up online redo log file is copied to a certain destination. This is called archiving and the copied file is called "archive log" file. "ARCn" processes are responsible for archiving the online redo log files.

40: What is an "External Procedure Call"?
Answer:

You can create a library (Dynamic Link Library (DLL) in windows or Shared Objects in Linux) for an operating system using C programming language. When developed according to certain structure and compiled with relevant Oracle Call Interface (OCI) libraries, it is possible to call the functions in these libraries from a PL/SQL code. This is called an "External Procedure Call". It is also possible to create a library using JAVA programming language and call it inside a PL/SQL code.

41: Where can it be useful to use an "External Procedure Call"?
Answer:

SQL (Structured Query Language) is ideal for set operations like retrieving rows, combining results etc. PL/SQL (Procedural Language) was developed to extend the capabilities of SQL. In PL/SQL, you can find common structures found in regular programming languages like if/then/else blocks or for loops. However, PL/SQL was developed to be a data manipulation language. It is not a fully capable programming language. You cannot do everything you want with PL/SQL or SQL. When such a need arises, you will need to use a more flexible and

capable programming languages like C or JAVA. You can
create libraries using JAVA or C and use them as external
procedure calls inside PL/SQL.

Also you may prefer to use a C library for performance
reasons. C is a low-level language and calculation intensive
operations will complete faster than PL/SQL because PL/SQL is
a higher level language. C binaries are directly executed in the
processor while PL/SQL code works in database domain.

42: What are the types of processes in an Oracle environment?

Answer:

There are three main types of processes in an Oracle
environment.

a) **Client Processes**: This is the process on the client side
that makes a connection to the database. This process
will usually be on a separate machine but it can also be
on the same server with the database.

b) **Server Processes**: This process is created for executing
the SQL requests coming from the clients. These
processes perform the actual work coming from users.

c) **Background Processes**: These are the system related
processes and required for the database itself to work.

**43: What is the duty of "Process Monitor" (PMON) process in
an Oracle database instance?**

Answer:

The PMON has two duties. One is to monitor server processes

and perform a process recovery if required. For example a server process might crash and terminate abnormally in the middle of a transaction. In such a situation the PMON process will detect crashed process, rollback the transaction that the process started, release any locks and will remove the process name from the list of active processes.

Another duty of PMON process is to register the service in configured listeners. Every 60 seconds, PMON will carry the service information to the configured listeners. This is called "service registration".

44: What are the two Manageability Monitor background processes and what do they do?

Answer:

There two background processes that are listed as manageability monitor processes. They are Manageability Monitor Process (MMON) and Manageability Monitor Lite Process (MMNL).

The **Manageability Monitor Process (MMON)** is mainly responsible for Automatic Workload Repository related tasks like taking snapshots at the configured periods, storing the statistics in AWR and producing alerts when a metric's threshold is violated.

The **Manageability Monitor Lite Process (MMNL)** is responsible for writing the contents of Active Session History (ASH) to disk. The ASH region resides on RAM in System Global Area and when that area gets full, the contents are written to database.

45: How does Oracle execute scheduler jobs and which background processes take part in this?

Answer:

The scheduled jobs are managed by "Oracle Scheduler". The information about the scheduled jobs is stored in JOB$ table. The "Oracle Scheduler" spawns a Job Coordinator (CJQ0) process to run the jobs. This process is the coordinator. It will monitor the JOB$ table to see if there is any job waiting to be run. The coordinator will then spawn "job queue slave processes" named "Jnnn" to execute the scheduled tasks. These background processes work dynamically. They may enter sleep state when they are idle or they might completely be shut down if they remain idle for a certain time. They will be re-spawned later when needed in the future.

This page is intentionally left blank.

Chapter 5

Patches and Upgrades

46: Suppose that an 11.2.0.2 database supports several applications, each with its own schema. Can you upgrade one of those schemas to 11.2.0.4 keeping the rest on the older version, to support policy requirements?

Answer:

No. The schemas share the version of the database and the software. When you apply a patch, or do a release upgrade, the entire database is affected and moves to the new version. It isn't possible to have different versions of software in the same database.

47: What are the names of the two scripts that are executed as a part of the manual upgrade procedure?

Answer:

The answer is catproc.sql and catalog.sql. These scripts are responsible for recreating the data dictionary, the dynamic performance views and preparing all the needed scripts, functionalities and packages for running PL/SQL on the database.

48: How do you apply a patch to a database? Where do you get the file, what are the generic steps and what is the name of the command to perform the actual task?
Answer:
The patches are obtained from the Oracle Support Page. The generic steps are, downloading the file, unzipping the file, changing the directory to the extracted folder, running the prerequisite checks and using the opatch utility with the command opatch apply.

Chapter 6

Database External Utilities

49: How do you use datapump to import a dumpfile from a database on server A to a different database on server B?

Answer:

DataPump cannot be used to import/export files from different servers. For that you need to use the older Exp/Imp utilities. DataPump can only send data directly via dblink between different databases on different servers.

50: You have a CSV file that you wish to load in a table. Which Oracle utility can you use for this?

Answer:

The utility is named SQLLoader. This is a utility supplied by Oracle and comes with the software to load external files into a database with a minimum amount of processing. It can be used on a schedule or ad-hoc.

51: What utility do you use to change the DBID? Why would you do this?

Answer:

You can use the NID utility. It can be used to change the database name as well as the DBID. This is useful, for example, for registering restored databases in a recovery catalog without conflicting with other databases and backups.

Chapter 7

Sessions and Processes

52: If a database has reached its maximum number of allowed processes, how can you increase this value?

Answer:

Access to the database is blocked since no new connections are possible, not even local. Some processes with LOCAL=NO must be killed in order to allow logging in the database. After this, you can increase the PROCESSES parameter, or you can kill sessions from within the DB or the OS.

53: A user contacts you saying that an update is taking too long. You check and find there is a session blocking the table with a wait of "SQL*Net message from client". Is this a problem?

Answer:

That wait means that the session is idle and its status will be "INACTIVE". The session finished the work and is waiting for commands. Probably the user simply opened a transaction, did not commit the changes and left his session open. You can either contact the user of the blocking session, or kill the session and it will rollback any changes.

54: You run top (or topas in AIX or process explorer in windows) and find that the process ID 10020 is consuming CPU for the last hour. How can you find the session SID of the corresponding session in the database?
Answer:

To find the corresponding session you need the V$process and V$session dynamic performance views. You join them by the v$process.addr and v$session.paddr columns and use as a predicate the v$process.spid column with the value 10020 and select the sid column on v$session.

55: You have an application server named "SPARC12" in your organization. You want to find users who are currently connected to from that server. How would you do that?
Answer:

I would query the V$SESSION view to find those users. I would run the query below:
sql> SELECT * FROM v$session WHERE machine='SPARC12' AND type='USER';
The "machine" column shows the name of the machine where the user is connected from. In this example it is "SPARC12" so I added the expression " machine='SPARC12' "

The "type" column shows the type of the session. It will be "BACKGROUND" for system session and it will be "USER" for regular non-system user connections.

56: In your organization, the application developers use SQL Developer program to connect to database. You want to find out the database username of the developers who are currently connected with SQL Developer. Write an SQL query for this.

Answer:

I would write the query below which queries v$session view.
SELECT username FROM v$session WHERE program='SQL Developer';

In this query, the "username" column shows the username of the connected users but we don't want to see the username of all the users in the database. We need to do a filtering on the users who are connected with "SQL Developer" program. The "program" column shows the operating system name of the program of the client so I add the phrase "WHERE program='SQL Developer' " to find the users who are connected with "SQL Developer" program.

57: You know that one of the employees in the company is connected to the database. His username in the active directory of the company is "joe.black" and the domain name of your company is "grey". Write a query to find the name of the computer that this user is connected from and port of the

physical connection.

Answer:

I would write the query below which queries v$session view.

sql> SELECT machine,port FROM v$session WHERE osuser= '
grey\joe.black';

This query retrieves the "machine" and "port" columns from
the v$session view. The "machine" column shows the name of
the computer that the client is connected from. "Port" column
shows the port of the physical network connection that is
between client and database server.

We also do a filtering here according to the "osuser" column.
The "osuser" column shows the username of the operating
system user which the client program runs under. The domain
name is "grey" and the domain username is "joe.black" so the
"osuser" column should show "grey\joe.black".

58: Explain what the below query is retrieving.

**sql> SELECT command,status FROM v$session WHERE
username='SCOTT';**

Answer:

This command queries v$session view which shows
information about the users connected to the database.

It does a filtering on the "username" column which shows the
username of the database user. In this example it is looking for
the specific user named "SCOTT".

The query retrieves "command" and "status" columns.

The "command" column shows an integer which corresponds

to the type of the command (SELECT,INSERT, UPDATE etc.) being executed.

The "status" column shows the status of the session like "ACTIVE, INACTIVE, KILLED" etc.

59: You want to disconnect all the users of your CRM application. You know that the database username of that CRM application is CRM2014. How would you disconnect all users of that application while the rest of the database remains fully operational?

Answer:

First I would find the session id and serial number of the sessions of that application. The below query will do that.

sql> SELECT sid,serial# FROM v$session WHERE username='CRM2014';

The "sid" column returns the session ids and "serial#" column returns the serial number for that session. Now you have a list of session ids and serial numbers of the session that you want to disconnect. Execute the command below for each session you've detected.

sql> alter system kill session '190,7' immediate;

The above command kills the session whose id is 190 and serial number is 7. Repeat this step for each session.

60: The server administrator says that he has detected an operating system process which consumes large memory and high CPU. If the server administrator gives you the process

id, can you find which session this process belongs to?

Answer:

Yes it is possible to track a process by its process id and find the corresponding session from it.

First you need to query the v$process view to find information about this specific process. For example, if the process id is 132 then execute the query below.

sql> SELECT addr FROM v$process WHERE spid=132 ;

This command retrieves the process address of that specific process. Let's say the query returned "000007FF3B87ADA8".

Now execute the command below:

sql> SELECT * FROM v$session WHERE paddr='000007FF3B87ADA8';

The command will return information about the session associated with that process. The "paddr" column shows the process address of the process of a session.

Chapter 8

Schemas and Schema Objects

61: In 11gr2, to use the UTL_FILE package what kind of database objects do you need to create to allow access to the filesystem?

Answer:

You need to create an Oracle Directory object. This allows access to the underlying directory based on the grants awarded to the user. Most common privileges are READ and WRITE. This is because the utl_file_dir should not be set to '*' which is a security breach.

62: You have two indexes on a table: on column A and a compound index on column A,B. Does a query on column B choose any of these indexes column B use?

Answer:

It doesn't use any indexes because the order of the compound index is A,B and not B,A. So the optimizer cannot use the index for lookups. You need to either rewrite your query, or create a new index (at least) on column B.

63: You as user A, need to access table LOGS in user B's schema. User B grants you select on the table, but when you run SELECT COUNT(1) FROM LOGS you receive a table doesn't exist error. Why?

Answer:

You need to prefix the table with the owner B.LOGS or you need to create a synonym LOGS for B.LOGS. Without this, the DB cannot find the table and reports an error.

64: What is the relationship between a schema and a user in an Oracle database?

Answer:

A database schema is a logical concept. It shows the collection of database objects like tables, indexes, views etc.

A database user has a username and a password. He logs on to the database with his username and password. A user is granted privileges to perform certain operations.

In an Oracle database, the database user owns a schema. The schema name and the username must be identical. A user can only own a single schema.

It is the schema that actually holds data and other objects. The user owns the schema. The user doesn't directly contain the objects.

65: List the object types that a schema can contain in an Oracle database.

Answer:

a) Tables

b) Indexes

c) Views

d) Sequences

e) Partitions

f) Dimensions

g) Synonyms

h) PL/SQL programs like procedures, functions and packages.

From the list of possible schema objects the most common ones are tables, indexes and PL/SQL programs.

The tables hold the actual data as rows and columns. The indexes are special structures which are used to speed up the access to tables. With the PL/SQL programs like procedures, you can write database programs and manipulate data.

66: How are schema objects stored logically? What is the relationship between these logical structures?

Answer:

Schema objects in an Oracle database which contain data are stored in logical structures called "segments". For example a table or indexes are actually segments in a schema because they hold data. Table holds data and indexes store the keys pointing to the rows in tables.

Segments are stored in another logical structure called tablespaces. A segment can belong to only one tablespace but a tablespace can contain one or more segments.

A schema can contain segments that are stored in different tablespaces.

67: How is a "view" stored in an Oracle database and how does it differ than the way a "table" is stored?

Answer:

Both "tables" and "views" are schema objects. Tables contain data as rows and columns. For example employees table holds the data of employees in an application. On the other hand a view doesn't contain data. A view is just a text of an SQL query. It can be viewed as a metadata.

A table contains a segment and this segment is contained in one of the tablespaces that the schema owner has access. However, a view is stored in data dictionary of a database in SYSTEM tablespace. A user can create a view even if he doesn't have privilege on any tablespace.

68: How are the schema objects stored physically? What is the relationship between these physical structures?

Answer:

a) The minimum physical storage unit is a "data block" in a database. Each data block in a tablespace has the same size. The default data block size is 8K. You can create tablespaces with different data block sizes than 8K. A data block can belong to only one object.

b) Data blocks form an extent. Extents are continuous data blocks. The number of continuous data blocks varies according to the size of the extent. An extent can belong to only one object and it cannot span multiple data files.

c) Data files are physical files that are stored on disk. Data files are composed of extents physically. An extent cannot span multiple data files. But logically a segment can be composed of multiple extents and a segment can span multiple data files.

69: What is schema object dependency? How does this mechanism work?

Answer:

The schema objects can be dependent on another schema. It can be even dependent on more than one object.

For example, a view can be a SELECT query which retrieves data from multiple tables. In such a situation, the view is called a "dependent object" on tables and the tables are called "referenced objects".

If somehow a referenced object becomes unusable, the dependent object will not work either. It will be marked as "invalid". For example, if you drop one of the underlying tables, the dependent view cannot return a result because of the missing table.

70: What are the administrative schemas in an Oracle Database?

Answer:

There are two administrative accounts in Oracle. "SYS" and "SYSTEM". They are created automatically when a database is created so they will exist in all databases.

These administrative accounts are for administrative tasks like starting and stopping the database, configuring the database, memory management etc.

SYS is a more privileged user than SYSTEM user.

These schemas contain regular schema objects like tables, indexes, views etc. The schema objects are required for an Oracle database to operate. They are created automatically during installation and should not be modified even by DBAs until suggested by Oracle support.

71: What is a sample schema? What are the sample schemas that can be installed?

Answer:

The sample schemas are regular schemas created by Oracle. They can be created during database creation or they can be installed later.

These schemas contain schema object to demonstrate Oracle features. You can use them for educational purposes. The most commonly used two sample schemas are below:

a) **HR**: This is called "Human Resource" schema. It is about an imaginary human resource application. It

demonstrates basic Oracle objects. For example it
contains tables like employees, departments, jobs etc.

b) **OE**: This is called "Order Entry" schema. This is a more
complex schema than HR and it is about an imaginary
Sales application. There are tables like customers,
products, orders etc.

72: What are the three types of tables according to the way the rows are organized?

Answer:

a) **Heap-Organized Tables**: This default table type. In a
heap-organized table, Oracle will insert rows where it
finds an empty space in the segment. The rows will not
be stored as sorted. When you execute a SELECT query,
the rows will return unsorted. However, you can still
use the SQL's "ORDER BY" clause to explicitly sort the
rows once they are read from the disk.

b) **Index-Organized Tables**: In this type of tables, the rows
are stored sorted according to the primary key of the
table. You might gain performance benefits for certain
scenarios with index-organized tables.

c) **External Tables**: You can present a text file (for
example: a comma separated value file) stored on disk
outside the database as a table. If configured
successfully, you can execute SQL queries on this text
file as it were a regular table in the database.

73: What is the difference between a "permanent table" and a "temporary table"?

Answer:

The "permanent table" is the default. Whatever you write into it, is stored on disk so it is persistent. Other session will also see the data you write in your session.

However, the "temporary table" is different. What you write into is not persistent. You won't see what you write into it, in another session. The data will be lost.

There are two types of temporary tables according to the lifetime of the data. One is transaction long and other is session long. If the lifetime of the data is transaction long, the data will disappear after the transaction ends (for ex: when you issue a commit.) If the lifetime of the temporary table is session long, the data will persist during your session. The data will disappear when you disconnect from the database.

74: What is the minimum information required to create a table?

Answer:

While creating a table, you need to determine a table name first. Every table has a unique name inside the schema.

A table is composed of one or more columns. For each column, you need to specify a column name and a data type. The column name has to be unique inside the table. However, there can be columns with the same name inside different tables in the same schema. The data type of the schema determines the type of the data that can be stored inside that column. For example, if the data type of the column is "number", you cannot store "text" in that.

75: You have reached a table of a web application. What objects can be expected to be found on this table?
Answer:

First, I expect to find indexes. Indexes are very common on tables. They keep keys and pointers to the rows containing that key. They speed up access to the data. They can also be used to enforce uniqueness.

I also expect to find referential integrity constraints. Columns may reference other column on another table or even on the same table. They enforce a parent-child relationship.

We can also find triggers created on that table. Triggers are code snippets which are fired when a certain event (ex: insert/delete/update) occurs on that table.

76: What kind of constraints can you define on a column?
Answer:

a) **Unique Constraint**: This guarantees that the values in the column will be unique.

b) **Not-Null Constraint**: This constraint guarantees that the values in the column will have a value. It cannot be left blank.

c) **Foreign Key Constraint**: The values on the column, references another column in the same table or in

another table. If there is no matching value on the
referenced column, then this constraint will be violated.

d) **Check Constraint**: In this constraint, you can check the
value according to defined rules. For example, "is value
greater than 3?"

77: Explain a physical table in an Oracle Database in terms of Logical Data Modeling.

Answer:

A physical table corresponds to an "entity" in logical model.
For example an "employee" might be an "entity" in logical
model and there can be a table named "EMPLOYEES" in the
database to hold information of the employees.

Columns in a table correspond to "attributes" in an entity. For
example there may be columns like
"first_name","last_name","date_of_birth" etc. These
correspond to attributes of the entity "employees".

The data type of the columns corresponds to "domains" in a
logical model. For example first_name of the column will be
varchar2 in a table and this will show the "domain" of the
attribute "first_name".

78: How does the character set affect a database?

Answer:

A regular table in the database will have columns with
"character" type data type. For example, it will have a column
with "varchar2" data type. The character set of the database

shows the character set of these columns.

For database, everything is a series of 1s and 0s which show a number. According to the character set, these numbers are mapped to a character. For example, if the character set of a text is Latin-1, the number 65 will correspond to the letter "A". The data in the system table space is stored in the character set of the database.

79: Explain the difference between "byte semantics" and "character semantics" in a table.

Answer:

A "text" in a computer is actually a series of bits. 8 bits form a "byte".

If a character type column is defined according to "byte semantics", the text is treated as a sequence of bytes. If a character type column is defined according to "character semantics", the text is treated as a sequence of characters. Let's say a column has a column with varchar2(100) data type. If the column uses byte semantics it means there can be maximum 100 bytes in this column. If the database uses a character set where each character is presented with two bytes then this column can hold maximum 50 characters.

80: Explain the "varchar2" data type and how it differs from a "char" data type.

Answer:

The "varchar2" means variable character. The length of the

column is not fixed. But you set an upper limit. For example if a column is created as varchar2(50), this means it will store maximum 50 characters in a single-byte character set database. However, you can also store a text which is shorter than 50 characters. For example if you store "foo" in that column, the length of the column will be 3.

In a "char" data type, the length of the column is fixed. For example, if you store "foo" in a column, then the length of the column will still be 50 because oracle will pad the text with blank until it reaches the length of the column.

81: What are the NVARCHAR2 and NCHAR data types?
Answer:

The letter "N" stands for "national". The NVARCAR2 is a variable-length character data type. It is same with the varchar2 data type except that it stores Unicode characters. The NCHAR is also similar to CHAR data type where the column length is fixed. Again the only difference between a CHAR data type and NCHAR data type is that the NCHAR column stores Unicode characters.

Unicode is a universal character set where any character in any alphabet can be stored. Its length is 2 bytes.

82: If you want to store the time zone data along with the date, which data types can you use in a column?
Answer:

There are two data types which also hold which time zone the date belongs to. These data types are "TIMESTAMP WITH LOCAL TIME ZONE" and "TIMESTAMP WITH TIME ZONE". These data types are also date types but they also hold zone information. The "TIMESTAMP WITH LOCAL TIME ZONE" stores the data in database's time zone and "TIMESTAMP WITH TIME ZONE" data type can store the time in any time zone.

When a client queries the data in these columns, the dates are converted to the time zone of the client before it is sent to client so different clients will see different values.

83: What is a rowid? What does a rowid show?
Answer:

A row id is a value which shows the physical location of a row in a table. It is stored according to a certain format that can be read by the database but it actually is a combination of the data file number, data block number and row number. Using these three pieces of information you can locate a row physically on disk.

The data file number shows the id of the data file that the row is stored. The data block number points to the data block inside that data file which holds the row. Finally, the row number shows the position of the row inside that block. A data block may hold more than one row and that row number shows the order of the row inside that data block.

84: Explain the "rowid" and "rownum" pseudo columns.

Answer:

In your queries, you can query "rowid" and "rownum" columns as if they existed.

For example: "Select rowid,rownum,first_name from tbl_employees".

Although there is no physical column named "rowid" and "rownum" on the table "tbl_employees", values will still be returned from those columns. That's why it is called pseudo columns.

The rowid column retrieves the rowid of the row which is a pointer to the physical location of the row on the disk. The rownum column retrieves the order of the row in the query. For example the rownum will be 1 for the first row, 2 for the second etc.

85: Explain why indexes are used so commonly and how they work.

Answer:

Indexes speed up access to data in a table. When you do a search on a column, if there is no index on that column, database needs to scan the entire table and compare each value with the value that is being searched. This operation will take a long time in large tables.

Indexes are secondary data structure in a table. They only store a "key" and a "rowid". The key is the value in the column being indexed. Rowid is a pointer to the row containing that key.

The key and rowids are stored in a special data structure called B*tree (Balanced tree). With the help of a b-tree, the database can find the sought key with a couple of movement. This is much more faster when compared with scanning the entire table.

86: Under what circumstances would it be a good idea to use indexes?

Answer:

It would be a good idea to use indexes under three conditions:

a) The column is used frequently in WHERE clauses in the SQL queries and the values sought are evenly distributed. The index is used to speed up queries.

b) You want to put a "not null" constraint on the column. An index will be created implicitly even if you don't create an index. In a "not null" constraint, the index is used to enforce the integrity.

c) It is a good idea to create an index on the foreign key column. Even if the foreign key column is not present in a query, while inserting a row or deleting a row from the parent table, the foreign key columns will be sought to find if the operation violates the foreign key constraint.

87: What is the difference between a usable index and an invisible index?

Answer:

If you mark an index as "unusable" it won't be maintained by DML operations. For example, it won't be updated when you add a row into the table and the index structure will be dropped by the database. Only the name and description of the index will remain.

However, if you make an index as "invisible" it will still be updated by the DML operations but the optimizer will ignore it. The optimizer will behave as there was no index on the column. Later, when you enable the index, the optimizer will start using the index.

88: What are reverse key indexes and why are they used?

Answer:

In a regular index, the values in the indexed columns are stored directly as a key in the index structure. For example, if the value in the column is "foo" then this value will be stored as "foo" as a key in the index. In reverse key indexes, the values are kept as reversed in the index. For example, the value "foo" in the column will be stored as "oof" in the index.

The reverse key indexes can be used spread the consequent values over many data blocks and they are most useful in sequence keys.

89: What is descending index and why would it be a good idea to use it?

Answer:

In a B*tree index, the index keys and the rowids are stored in a Balanced Tree Structure. The balanced tree is a special structure where the values are stored in "leaves" and the leaves store the values as sorted in ascending order.

When you search a key in an index, you start from the top branch and move to the sub branches according to the values. You usually reach the sought leave in 3 moves.

In your select queries, if you query the indexed column in ascending order, the database will just read the keys from the beginning to the end.

A descending index key is the same with a regular B*tree index except that the keys are stored in reverse-order.

90: What is a function-based index and where should it be used?

Answer:

In a regular index, the values in the indexed column are stored in the index and in queries the values are sought in the index. But the developer may not use the column directly. Instead, he may use a function. Ex:

sql> Select * from employees where upper(first_name)='JOE';

The optimizer cannot use the index in the above query because the relevant key in the index might be "Joe". The developer has used the function "UPPER".

In such situations, to be able to use the index, you need to create function-based indexes. In a function-based index, the value in the column is not directly stored in the index, instead the output of the function is used. In this example, the key in the index will be "JOE".

91: When should you choose bitmap indexes over B*tree indexes?

Answer:

There are situations where it would be preferable to use Bitmap indexes over regular B*tree indexes.

a) If the distribution of the values is not even in the column it might be a good idea to use bitmap indexes. For example, if the column that you want to index is holding GENDER information, it will have only two values. This column is a good candidate for a bitmap index.

b) The column should also not be updated frequently. The maintenance cost of a bitmap index is high so the column should be either read-only or rarely updated.

92: What is a view as a schema object?

Answer:

A view is actually a stored SELECT query. You can write an SQL that retrieves rows from different tables and store it as a view.

After that, the developers might directly write queries on that view as it were a regular table. But unlike a regular table, a view has no segment. It doesn't actually store any data. It is just a definition and the definition itself is stored in the data dictionary of the database.

93: What is the force option used for when creating a view?
Answer:

A view itself is a schema object but it doesn't have a segment which means it doesn't contain any data. It is just a definition of an SQL "select" query. The "select" query can read a single table, join multiple tables, do projection or use a predicate (WHERE clause). The "select" query has to be a valid query. All the underlying tables that the query references should exist. Otherwise you cannot create the view. However, sometimes you may want to create the view even though some of the base tables do not exists. In this case, you have to create the view with "force" option. When you use force option, the view will be created anyway.

94: Explain why it would be a good idea to use a view?
Answer:

a) **To hide the complexity of underlying tables**. The view might perform joins from many tables but it will appear as a single table to the developers.

b) **Provide More Granular Security**: You can create a view which only select a few columns of a table and grant SELECT privileges on that view to users. This way, the users won't have SELECT privilege on the entire base table but to only a portion of it.

c) **Minimize the effect of structural changes**: You can configure your applications to use the view instead of the tables directly. Later if you change the name of a column, you can still you an alias in the view instead of the original name, so that the developers won't have to change their existing code.

95: What is a materialized view and how does it differ from a regular view?

Answer:

A regular view is only a definition of a SELECT query. It only contains the SQL text in the data dictionary. It has no segment and it doesn't store any data.

A materialized view also has a definition which is still an SQL query but this time the materialized view has a segment and the result of the SQL query is stored in that segment.

When a user queries a regular view, he is directed to the underlying tables to retrieve data. However, when a user queries a materialized view, he directly retrieves the data in the Materialized view segment. The user doesn't read the base tables.

96: What is the difference between a "complete refresh" and a "fast refresh" in materialized views?

Answer:

If you're using a materialized view, you'll usually want to refresh it with latest data. You have two options here:

a) **Complete Refresh**: All the data in the materialized view segment is deleted and all the data in the SELECT query is inserted again from scratch.

b) **Fast Refresh**: In this option, a "materialized view log" is created on the schema where base tables are stored. Oracle creates to track DML operations on the base tables. All the changes made to base tables are recorded in the Materialized View Log. When you start a fast refresh, only the recorded changes are applied. Not the whole result is carried.

97: How are the sequences incremented in Oracle?

Answer:

Sequences increment by one as a default. You can also define your own increment amount. For example you may configure the sequence to increment by 3.

The value of the sequence increase when its "nextval" method is used in a referenced in a query. For example the below query will increment the sequence.

sql> select my_sequence.nextval from dual;

Once a sequence is incremented, it is not possible to decrease it again. It will still keep its incremented value even if is used in a transaction and that transaction is rolled back.

98: How would you select the current value of a sequence and how does this method behave for concurrent separate sessions?

Answer:

You can read the current value of a sequence inside a query. Sequences have a method named "currval" which will return the current value of the sequence when it is called. Below is a sample query to read the current value of the sequence named "my_sequence".

sql> select my_sequence.currval from dual;

This method only returns the current value of the sequence since the last call of the "nextval" method in your session. It is not the global current value of the sequence. Other sessions in the database might have incremented it in the meantime. The "currval" won't show it. Its scope is your session only.

99: Why would you want to use the CACHE feature of sequences?

Answer:

The sequences increment as their "nextval" method is called. This will increment the sequence by one as a default. But the sequence might have a non-default increment amount. This is determined during sequence creation.

Sequences are schema objects and they can be referenced by multiple concurrent session in the database. A typical use of a sequence is primary keys in tables like employee id, transaction id etc.

If you have a busy database that heavily utilizes sequences, you may have performance problems. For such configurations, Oracle allows to "cache" the specific number of next values of a sequence in memory. For example if you create the sequence with "cache 15" then the next 15 values of the sequence is kept in system global area (SGA). Accessing the next values will be faster if cached, because they will be pre-computed. Otherwise the computation of the next values will be performed in your session which might degrade performance for busy databases.

100 : You have an "employees" table in your application. You want to assign an employee id which will uniquely identify each employee. You want the employee id to increment by one and you don't want any gap between two employee ids. The developer thinks that it would be improper to use a sequence to accomplish task. Explain why it will be a bad idea to use a sequence here.

Answer:

At a first glance, using sequences might seem ideal for such a requirement where you're going to assign a unique ID to each employee. You may create a sequence which increments by one and call it each time you insert a record into the employees table. This would work.

But there is one more condition which makes the use of sequences impractical. There is a requirement to prevent gaps. Sequences will be improper. Because, in the transaction where you'll insert a row into the "employees" table, you'll reference the "nextval" method of the sequence and the transaction might rollback if an error occurs. Even if the transaction is rolled back, the sequence won't rollback. There is no way to revert the sequence to its original state. This makes the use of a sequence improper for this requirement.

101: Explain the "synonym" schema object.

Answer:

Synonyms are schema objects but they don't have a segment. They don't contain data like views. They only have definitions which are kept in the data dictionary.

A synonym is a label which can be used instead of the original object name. If the object name is long or is not descriptive, you may create a synonym which will be short and descriptive for the underlying object name. You can directly use this synonym instead of the original object name in your queries. The synonym will be translated into the original object name implicitly.

102: What is the difference between a private synonym and a public synonym?

Answer:

The main difference lies in the scope of these objects. Private synonyms are schema objects and they belong to a schema. Their scope is the schema they reside under.

On the other hand, a public synonym is global within the database. Its scope is the whole database. They don't belong to a single schema. Any user in the database can reference it in their applications. However, this doesn't mean that every user will have access to the underlying object. They just have access to the synonym which will translate into the underlying object name.

103: Explain where it would be a good idea to use synonyms and give examples for them.

Answer:

The synonyms are labels which can be used instead of original object names. The synonyms are regular schema objects. It is a good idea to use the synonyms in two situations:

First, the original object name might not be descriptive. We usually want the object names to be descriptive for ease of use in code. For example let's say there is a table name named "T_TRNS PRDC_LST" which holds the list of the transactions for the products. Instead of this object name, you might create a synonym "T_PRODUCT_TRANSACTION_LIST" for this table. Another scenario, where it would be a good idea to use synonym is objects referenced in another database via a db link. In such a situation the object name will be long and not neat. For example to reach a table named "PRODUCTS" under "ORDERENTRY" schema via a database link named "DB_LINK_DR.NEWYORK", you'll need to write:

sql> select * from ORDERENTRY.PRODUCTS@ DB_LINK_DR.NEWYORK;

Instead of writing this for each time you want to access this table, you might create a synonym named just "products" for "ORDERENTRY.PRODUCTS@ DB_LINK_DR.NEWYORK;"

This page is intentionally left blank.

Chapter 9

Data Integrity

104: What are the techniques at a database level to guarantee data integrity to avoid application issues?

Answer:

You can validate user input / new records by using Triggers, Database Constraints and Foreign Keys.

105: What is a "NOT NULL" constraint and where is it used?

Answer:

"Not Null" constraints are created on a table inside a schema. Columns in a table may contain null values as a default. However, you'll want to enforce some columns to contain values and prevent them from being NULL.

The "NOT NULL" constraints are used for this purpose. It is an integrity constraint. If you create a "not null" constraint for a column and you don't set a value for that column inside insert and update statements, the database will raise an error and your transaction will be rolled back. This is how Oracle enforces the data integrity.

106: What is a "unique constraint" and why would you need that?

Answer:

A "unique constraint" guarantees that a column or a combination of multiple columns will be unique inside a table. For example, you have a "customers" table. This table has a "phone_number" column which stores the phone numbers of the customers. You want this column to be unique inside the table. Here, you need to create a unique key constraint on the "phone_number" column. In such a situation, if a customer tries to insert a phone number which already resides in that column, Oracle will raise an error. This way, the uniqueness of "phone_number" column is satisfied. The constraint will be forced for all insert and update statements.

107: What is a primary key? Where is it used?

Answer:

A primary key is an integrity constraint. There can be only one primary key on a table. It uniquely identifies a row in that table. It can be created on a column or a combination of multiple columns.

Once a primary key constraint is created on a column then that column will have to be unique and that column cannot be left null. This way, it is guaranteed that the primary key will identify each row uniquely.

Oracle will create a unique index implicitly, once you define a primary key. This is how the constraint is applied physically.

108: What is the difference between a primary key constraint and a unique key constraint?

Answer:

These two integrity constraints are similar but not identical.

A unique key constraint guarantees that all the values on the column will be unique. No duplicate values will be allowed. But, that column might have null values in it. The null may be found multiple times.

A primary key constraint guarantees that the values in the column will be unique and each row will have a value. No nulls will be accepted. This is the main difference.

There can be only one primary key constraint on table; however, there can be multiple unique key constraints on a table.

109: What is a "natural key" and a "surrogate key"? What is the difference between these two?

Answer:

The application developers will do data modeling according to the business rules. The data modeling will represent the entities in the real world.

For example, in the logical model you'll have "employees". Every employee will have attributes like "first name", "last name" , "gender" etc. The logical "employees" entity will correspond to physical "employees" table and the logical attributes will correspond to columns.

A natural key is an attribute or a collection of attributes that would naturally identify an entity. For example, social security id of an employee can be an example of a natural key.

A surrogate key is a key which you produce yourself to identify each row uniquely. It is imaginary. For example, you may produce a unique number "employee id" for each employee yourself and use it as the primary key.

110: What is a foreign key constraint?

Answer:

A foreign key constraint is created for a column and it references a unique key on another table or in the same table. The foreign key constraint guarantees that there will be an occurrence of the column value in the referenced unique key constraint.

The referenced key can be either a unique key or a primary key. The referenced constraint is mandatory.

This constraint establishes a parent-child relation between two tables. The referenced table is the parent table and the other table is the child table.

The foreign key can also be defined for multiple columns. In such a case, the referenced key should also be a multiple column key and it should contain the same number of rows and same data types. The order of the columns should also match.

111: What are the options of cascade if a record in the parent table is deleted or updated?

Answer:

There are three options and these are set during the creation of the foreign key constraint.

    a) **No Action**: This is the default option. No action will be taken. However, delete/update operations will not be permitted if they violate the constraint.

    b) **Delete Cascade**: In this option, if a record is deleted from the parent table then the corresponding records in the child table will also be deleted to comply with the foreign key constraint violation.

    c) **Delete Set Null**: In this option, if a record is deleted from the parent table then the corresponding column in the child table will be set to NULL to comply with the foreign key constraint violation.

112: What can be done to improve performance and usability of foreign key constraints?

Answer:

When a record in the parent table is updated or deleted, the database will check if the foreign key constraint will be violated by this action. You need to create an index on the child table to improve performance. If you create an index, database will do an index access to check the violation. Otherwise, it will perform a full table scan which can degrade the performance seriously.

Database will also place a full table lock on the child table during this check if there is no index. If there is an index on the foreign key column then only the index will be locked. This improves usability of the index.

113: What is a check constraint?

Answer:

The check constraint is an integrity constraint. It is created on a table.

A check constraint checks the value of the one or more columns according to the desired logic and if it returns "true" the condition is met, otherwise the condition is not met and the integrity is violated.

A check constraint will be useful when you need a more flexible integrity constraint. For example you may create a check constraint where it checks whether the "salary" column in greater than 5000.

114: What is the difference between an "ENABLE VALIDATE" and "ENABLE NOVALIDATE" constraint?

Answer:

The first word "ENABLE" shows the state of for the future data. It means that the integrity constraint will be applied to the future data. When you perform insert/delete/update, the constraint will be checked against the upcoming data.

The second word (validate or invalidate) shows the state for the existing data on a table. While creating an integrity constraint, if you specify the "validate" option, the existing data will be checked against this constraint. If any row which violates the constraint if found, an error occurs and the constraint cannot be created.

On the other hand, if you specify "novalidate" option, the existing data will not be checked and the constraint will be created even if the existing data violates it.

115: Explain the difference between a "deferrable" constraint and a "non-deferrable" constraint.

Answer:

These two options determine the way the constraint check is performed.

In a transaction, you can execute more than one INSERT/DELETE/UPDATE statements. This is normal. In a non-deferrable constraint, the integrity constraint is checked after each single statement. If the constraint is violated, an error occurs immediately and the transaction is stopped.

In a deferrable constraint, the integrity constraint is checked at the end of the transaction when a commit occurs. The constraint is checked for all of the statements that has occurred inside that transaction.

This page is intentionally left blank.

Chapter 10

Data Dictionary and Dynamic Performance Views

116: As a DBA you want to know which objects on schema B does user A have privileges. Where do you go for this information?

Answer:

For this information you query the DBA_TAB_PRIVS table which contains a list of objects and the name of the user who has access to them.

117: A user reports that he has a query running for more than one hour. How do you find his session and what is the value of the TYPE column for his session?

Answer:

The DMV to check is V$session if on a single instance or GV$session if on RAC. The TYPE column will have a USER value and the LAST_CALL_ET column should be queried for a value bigger than 3600. This column refers to the duration in seconds of the current statement.

118: Explain what a "base table" and a "view" means in a data dictionary.

Answer:

The data dictionary itself has tables to store system related data. Oracle database needs these tables to operate. These are called base tables. Administrators should not need to access these tables under normal circumstances. The data itself might also be cryptic.

The data in the base tables are exposed to users via "views" in a data dictionary. These views decrypt the data and make it readable to outside.

For example, user$ is a base table and "dba_users" is a view in an Oracle database data dictionary.

119: What are the three prefixes that are seen in the data dictionary views?

Answer:

There prefixes can be seen in data dictionary views.

   a) **DBA_**: This prefix means that records for all the users will be returned in this view.
   b) **ALL_**: This prefix means that this view will return records for current user plus the records for data which the user has access at that moment.
   c) **USER_**: This prefix means that the view will return

records only for the objects owned by the current user. For example, the USER_TABLES view returns a list of tables owned by the current user, the ALL_TABLES returns a list of tables owned by the current user plus other tables which the user has access at that moment and finally DBA_TABLES view returns record for all the tables in the database.

120: What is the use of the "DUAL" table in the data dictionary?

Answer:

The DUAL table is a publicly accessible table. It can be accessed by any user in the database.

It has only one column named "DUMMY" and it has only one row which contains the value "X".

You can use this table in your queries where you need to return only one column and one row.

For example, you need to calculate 3+4 and return the result. You can use the DUAL table in such a situation.

sql> select 3+4 from dual;

121: What are dynamic performance views in a database?

Answer:

The dynamic performance views are virtual tables that are created when an instance is started. They are called dynamic performance views because they can be updated as the database is running.

The dynamic performance views start with the prefix "V$" and they are owned by the "SYS" user.

In a Real Application Cluster, most of the time there will be another view starting with "GV$". G stands for global and it contains records for each instance in the RAC. For example, V$SESSION view will show information about the current sessions in the instance where you're accessing the view and GV$SESSION will show information about the sessions in all the instances in the cluster.

Chapter 11

SQL

122: What parts can be found in a regular SELECT statement?

Answer:

a) **Projection**: This is the part where we define a set of columns to read from the table. * means all the columns will be selected.

b) **FROM**: This is the part where define a set of table or views which want to read data from.

c) **Predicate**: This is the part where we do filtering. This is also called "where" clause.

d) **Sorting**: This is the part where you can sort the result according to certain columns.

e) **Grouping**: This is the part where you can group the results according to certain columns.

123: Explain the DDL statements in SQL.

Answer:

DDL stands for data definition language.

a) The queries which change the properties of objects in a schema fall under the category DDL. For example creating an object, altering an object or dropping it are all categorized as data definition language.

b) Deleting rows from a table is not a DDL statement but "truncating" a table is a DDL statement because it alters the physical structure of table at background.

c) Granting a privilege or revoking a privilege is also considered to be DDL.

d) Enabling auditing or disabling auditing are also DDL statements.

124: What is DML in SQL?

Answer:

DML stands for data manipulation language. This is a category for SQL queries for SELECT/INSERT/DELETE/UPDATE statements.

a) **SELECT**: This statement is used for reading records from a table.

b) **INSERT**: This statement is used for inserting rows into a table.

c) **DELETE**: This statement is used for deleting rows from a table.

d) **UPDATE**: This statement is used for updating one or

more columns in a table.

The INSERT/DELETE/UPDATE statements start a transaction implicitly. The SELECT statement doesn't start a transaction. Explicitly locking a table with "LOCK TABLE" statement is also considered to a DML statement.

125: Explain the types of "joins" that can be found in an SQL statement.

Answer:

There are three types of joins that can be performed.

a) **INNER JOIN**: In this join, only the rows that satisfy the join condition is returned.

b) **OUTER JOIN**: This type of join can be divided into three categories. LEFT OUTER JOIN, RIGHT OUTER JOIN and FULL OUTER JOIN. In an outer join, the matching rows from the tables are returned plus the rows where there is not a matching value are also returned.

c) **CARTESIAN PRODUCT**: In this type of join, all rows from the all tables are returned without a join condition. The number of rows returned is the multiplication of the rows in the source tables.

126: What are the three types of outer joins?

Answer:

There are three types of outer joins. These are: right outer, left outer and full outer joins.

a) **Left Outer Join**: In this type of join, all matching rows plus the rows which don't satisfy the condition on left table are returned.

b) **Right Outer Join**: In this type of join, all matching rows plus the rows which don't satisfy the condition on right table are returned.

c) **Full Outer Join**: In this type of join, all matching rows plus the rows which don't satisfy the condition on both the right table and the left table are returned.

127: What is an implicit SELECT query?

Answer:

You can write SELECT queries and read data from tables. This is explicitly executing a SELECT query. You read the data and form the results.

You can also execute UPDATE or DELETE statements to update columns or delete rows of a table. These will be explicitly running UPDATE/DELETE queries. However, it is possible to do a selective UPDATE/DELETE using a "where" clause. Ex:

sql> delete from employees where emp_id=4;

For example, the above query deletes the rows in the employees table where emp_id equals 4. In this query an implicitly SELECT statement runs to find the rows where emp_id=4.

128: What are the Transaction Control Statements?

Answer:

It is possible to control the transaction flow explicitly by using some commands. These commands are called Transaction Control Statements (TCL).

a) **COMMIT**: This command commits the changes made inside that transaction and ends the transaction. The changes become permanent after a commit.

b) **ROLLBACK**: This command rolls back the changes made inside that transaction and ends the transaction.

c) **SAVEPOINT**: This command creates a point to which you can rollback.

d) **SET TRANSACTION**: This command is used for setting properties for the transaction.

e) **SET CONSTRAINT**: This command determines whether the constraints will be deferred or not.

129: Explain the Session Control Statements.

Answer:

A session starts when a user logs on to the database and lasts until the user logs off. A session implicitly ends if the server process of the session crashes. The database will end the session if it detects that the process is not present.

You can execute some commands and change the characteristic of a session with "ALTER SESSION". These commands are categorized as Session Control Statement.

You can also enable a role with "SET ROLE" command during

a session. This is also called as a session control statement.

130: Explain the most widely used access paths that the optimizer performs.

Answer:

a) **Full Table Scan**: The whole table is read from the beginning. This can degrade the performance critically.

b) **Rowid Scan**: The row is directly accessed using rowid. This is the fastest way as a rowid shows the location of the row on disk.

c) **Index Scan**: Index structure is accessed instead of the table. The sought value is first searched in the index leaves. An index also stores the rowid along with the keys. Once the sought key is found, database will read the relevant rowid and access the sought row using that rowid.

131: What are the four types of optimizer statistics?

Answer:

a) **Table Statistics**: This statistics show information about a table like how many rows there are, how many blocks does this table contain, how many data blocks are there for this table etc.

b) **Column Statistics**: This statistics show information about the columns like number of distinct values, number of null values, the distribution of values etc.

c) **Index Statistics**: This statistics show information about an index like how many leaves and blocks are there, what is the level of the index etc.

d) **System Statistics**: This statistics show information about the system hardware like CPU, I/O speed etc.

132: What is an "Optimizer Hint"?

Answer:

When you execute an SQL query, the optimizer will evaluate different paths to return the rows requested in the query. It is possible to return the same rows using different access paths. All paths will have a cost to return the rows. Optimizer will try to determine the path with the lowest cost.

However, it is possible instruct the optimizer to choose a specific path using directives called an optimizer hint. Optimizer hints are place between "/*+<optimizer_hint>*/" statements. For example you may write a hint to force the optimizer to use an existing index, if you are sure that it is the best way to use that index.

133: What are the three types of checks that are performed during SQL parsing phase?

Answer:

a) **Syntax Check**: At this step, the syntax of the query is checked. You can only use specific commands in an SQL query. For example, you can use "SELECT" but you cannot use "SELECTXX123". This will be detected at syntax check.

b) **Semantic Check**: At this step, the query is checked according to its meaning. For example you cannot read from a non-existent table in a query. This is detected at this phase.

c) **Shared Pool Check**: Once a query is parsed, the optimizer needs to create an execution plan. Optimizer will store this execution plan in library cache in the shared pool. The next time the same query is executed, the execution plan will directly be retrieved from shared pool not to lose time with the same path cost calculation. The checking of the execution plan in the shared pool is performed in the step.

Chapter 12

Programming

134: Explain how a client-side program interacts with an Oracle database.

Answer:

The client-side programming means the program is executed outside the database. The client-side program usually works in another computer like a separate application server or a workstation. You can write the program with a programming language like C, JAVA or .NET.

You'll need to use a driver to connect to the database and interact with the database. The programming languages will usually have built-in libraries to interact with Oracle.

You'll embed the SQL query in your application, the SQL query will be sent to database and the results will be returned to the client program.

135: What is the difference between a thin driver and a thick driver?

Answer:

Client-side programs need a driver to connect to the database. The driver will have the libraries that know how to interact with Oracle. The programming languages will usually have built-in Oracle libraries.

An Oracle driver is required to make a connection to Oracle, but some drivers require Oracle Client software to be persistent on the computer where they run. Such drivers are called "thick drivers".

Some drivers are fully Oracle aware and they don't need Oracle Client software to be present on the computer where they run. Such drivers are called "thin drivers".

136: Explain server-side programming.

Answer:

In a server-side programming, the code resides on the database server and directly executes inside the database. You can write server-side program using Oracle's PL/SQL or JAVA.

You can save the PL/SQL code inside a schema object like a package or procedure. When you call these objects, the PL/SQL code inside them will be executed. These objects can even be called from a client application. It doesn't matter. The PL/SQL code will be executed on the database.

You can also write code using JAVA and prepare a JAVA class. It is possible to run this java class on the database. The Oracle database has a built-in JVM to run JAVA classes.

137: What is Oracle Client Software and why is it needed?

Answer:

Oracle client software includes the libraries and programs to connect to an Oracle database. At the core of the client software lies the Oracle Call Interface library which is called OCI shortly.

The Oracle Call Interface is a dynamic library which you can include in your application. It has methods inside it, which you can call to interact with an Oracle database.

However, in most programming languages, you won't directly call this interface. These languages will have "wrapper" libraries which comply with the data types in that language. However, these wrapper libraries will call the actual OCI library found in the Oracle client.

138: Why would a stored PL/SQL program perform better than an anonymous PL/SQL block?

Answer:

First, in a stored program, the PL/SQL code will be stored on the database. In an anonymous PL/SQL code, that code has to be sent from the client to the server. For long code, that might cause slowness because of the extra network transportation step.

Second, the stored program is already compiled on the database. However, the anonymous code will have to be compiled first.

Third, the stored code is likely to be found in SGA if it was called by another session before. The database won't have to read it from disk. It will directly locate it on SGA.

139: In which schema objects can you store the PL/SQL code you've written?

Answer:

You can store your code as a standalone procedure. This way, you can directly call this procedure inside a schema.

Procedures will execute the code inside them but they won't return a value back to the caller.

You can store your code as a standalone function. The code in a function will be executed when the function is called and the function will return back a value to the caller.

You can store your code inside a package. A package will contain procedures and functions inside it.

Last, you can store it in a trigger. Triggers are created on tables and they are run when certain operation like insert/delete/update happen on that table.

140: List out three advantages that you can gain by using a PL/SQL package.

Answer:

Writing a PL/SQL package offers three main advantages. These are:

  a) **Encapsulation**: With the help of a PL/SQL package, you can group related stored procedures, function and data types in a named object. This also makes your program more organized.

b) **More Security**: There can be stored procedures and function inside a package and you can define which are public and which are private. Public procedures can be called by external sessions where private procedures can only be called inside another procedure inside the package.

c) **Better Development**: Other stored programs which use a package only reference the package specification. You can make changes inside a package body and recompile only the body without touching the specification. Referencing programs won't be affected as there will be no change in the specification.

141: What constructs can be found in a PL/SQL Code?
Answer:

a) **Variables and Constants**: These are the regular variables and constants you can find in a programming language. A variable is actually a pointer to an area in memory. They represent a value. Constants are fixed and they cannot be changed while the program is running.

b) **Cursors**: You can declare cursors inside a PL/SQL code and perform row-based operations. For example you can iterate inside the rows and update some columns in them.

c) **Exceptions**: You can define exception blocks inside a PL/SQL code. If an error rises during the execution of the code, the execution will jump to the exception block.

142: Why does working with batch collections perform better than working on a single record at a time?
Answer:

This is because of the architecture of an Oracle instance. There are separate engines for running an SQL query and a PL/SQL code. (SQL Engine and PL/SQL Engine)

A stored program can contain both PL/SQL code and SQL code. When running an SQL code, the server process switches to SQL engine and while executing a PL/SQL code, it switches to the PL/SQL engine.

If you process a collection one by one, the server process will constantly switch back and forth between SQL Engine and PL/SQL engine. This will decrease the performance.

By performing batch operations on collections, you decrease these switches, thus improve performance.

143: What events can fire a trigger in a database?
Answer:

a) **DML Operations**: You can create a trigger to be fired after an INSERT/DELETE/UPDATE operation on a table or view.

b) **DDL Operations**: You can create a trigger to be fired

after a DDL statement is executed by a user or any user.
For example you can write a trigger that will be fired
when somebody drops a table in the database.

c) **Database Events**: You can define triggers that will be
fired after certain database events. For example, when
database starts up, shuts down. etc.

144: Why would you use triggers in a database?

Answer:

You can use triggers to enforce data integrity when the
integrity logic is complex. You can use SQL and PL/SQL to
check some values and prevent DML on the table according to
that. The existing structures for enforcing data integrity
(foreign key constraints, primary key constraints, check
constraints etc.) are not much flexible. Triggers can provide the
flexibility you need.

You can also use triggers for auditing purposes. Oracle has a
built-in auditing mechanism which is quite useful. But again if
you need a more flexible auditing option, you can use triggers
to log the activities on tables.

145: What is the difference between a "row trigger" and a "statement trigger"?

Answer:

a) You can create a trigger as a row trigger or as a
statement trigger on a table. The code that will be
executed can even be the same. It doesn't matter.

b) A row trigger will fire for each row affected by the relevant DML statement. However, the statement trigger will only fire once for the relevant DML statement.

c) A row trigger will not be fired, if the DML statement doesn't affect any row. However, the statement trigger will be fired in anyway.

146: Explain the times when a trigger can be configured to run.

Answer:

You can create a trigger on a table and configure it to run at certain times. These timings are listed below in execution order:

a) **Before Statement**: This is valid for statement triggers and the triggers will be fired before the statement executes.

b) **Before Each Row**: This is valid for row triggers and the trigger will be fired before each row is processed.

c) **After Statement**: This is valid for statement triggers and the triggers will be fired after the statement executes.

d) **After Each Row**: This is valid for row triggers and the trigger will be fired after each row is processed.

147: When would it be a good idea to use "before" triggers? Explain with an example.

Answer:

The before triggers are ideal for enforcing data integrity. You can use triggers to enforce data integrity where regular integrity objects (primary keys, foreign keys, check constraint etc.) are not flexible enough to satisfy the integrity rule. Inside the trigger you can check if the statement satisfies the integrity condition and raise an error if it violates the integration rules. For example, you don't want any update operations to be executed on the "orders" table on Sundays. You can create a before statement trigger on the "orders" table. Inside the trigger, you check the current day. If it is Sunday, you can raise an exception and cause the statement to fail. This way you'll have prevented any DML on the table on Sundays.

148: When would it be a good idea to use "after" triggers? Explain with an example.

Answer:

The "after" triggers are ideal for auditing purposes.

Oracle has a built-in auditing mechanism. You can use this to audit certain activities like DML statements, DDL statements, GRANTs etc. These audit records provide information to track the activities.

However, you may want to implement your own auditing system when the built-in audits don't satisfy your needs.

For example, you may want to audit any DML activity on the "orders" table at weekend. You may create an after statement trigger for DML activities on the "orders" table. Inside the trigger, you can check the current day and if it is weekend, you can insert a record into your audit table for this.

Chapter 13

Data Concurrency and Consistency

149: User A is running a long uncommitted transaction with several DML statements on table Z. User B queries table Z 60 minutes after user A started and gets the 0RA-01555 error. What does this mean?

Answer:

The 01555 error indicates that user A's transaction ran for too long, and overwrote some data present before the start of user A's transaction required for a consistent view of the data on behalf of user B.

150: What is read consistency in an Oracle Database?

Answer:

When you start a SELECT statement, Oracle will show you the records at the time you started the query. For example, the query might take 5 minutes to complete. The data might change during that time. However, Oracle will show you the records how it was at the beginning of the query. This is called consistent reading.

If a data block changes while the query is running, Oracle produces the before image of the record using the undo records.

151: What is a dirty read? Explain with an example.

Answer:

When you start a SELECT query, database will start reading relevant records from the tables. For large result sets, the reading will take long.

During reading, other session might start a transaction which modifies the data in these data blocks. That transaction might have not committed yet. These are called dirty data because we don't know if the transaction will succeed (commit). The transaction might be rolled back.

In such a situation, if the database reads the uncommitted data and returns them in the results set, this is called a dirty read. This is usually not wanted. Oracle doesn't do dirty reads.

152: From the isolation levels, explain how "read committed" transactions behave?

Answer:

A transaction starts implicitly when a DML statement is executed in a session. Multiple statements might be executed until the transaction ends.

When a select query starts, it will start reading data blocks where the sought data resides. Depending on the size of the result set, this might take a long time and other transactions might have changed the data while the query is still running. In a "read committed" transaction, Oracle will show the results at the time the SELECT statement started. This is the default isolation level.

153: From the isolation levels, explain how "serializable" transactions behave?

Answer:

A transaction starts implicitly when a DML statement is executed in a session. Multiple statements might be executed until the transaction ends.

In a "serializable" transaction, all the SELECT queries will return rows as they were at the time the transaction began. Not the time the SELECT query began.

You can still make modification to data in a serializable transaction, but this data should not have been changed by another transaction after the current transaction began. Otherwise you'll get an error.

154: Explain how readers and writers interact with each other according to the row locking mechanism in Oracle.

Answer:

Oracle handles locking at row level. When a transaction makes a change to a row, that row is locked implicitly.

Once a row is locked by a writer, no other writers can modify the data in it until the lock is release. They will have to wait until the lock is released but readers can still read the locked row.

In Oracle, read operations won't block writers. You can update a row while it is being read by a query.

155: What is the difference between an exclusive lock and a shared lock?

Answer:

When an object is locked exclusively, no other sessions can alter that object until the exclusive locked is released. The first transaction which places an exclusive lock will be the owner of the object and other transactions will have to wait until the owner releases the lock.

In shared locks, a transaction may put a shared lock on the object and then another object might also place shared lock on the same object. If there is a shared lock on an object, you cannot place an exclusive lock on that object.

156: Tell us about the life time of an exclusive row lock and give an example.

Answer:

Most of the time the lock will be help during the life time of a transaction. For example, in your session you've updated some rows in a table. This will start a transaction implicitly. You'll have acquired an exclusive lock on the updated rows. These locks will only be released until the transaction ends. You may end the transaction explicitly by executing commit or rollback. The transaction might also implicitly be rolled back. For example, the server process that began the transaction might have crashed unexpectedly. The PMON process will detect this and release any relevant locks acquired by that transaction.

157: How does a deadlock occur? Explain with an example.

Answer:

When two transactions wait for the other to release a lock, a deadlock occurs. The deadlock will continue forever because both of the transactions will wait for the other side to finish first. Let's give an example:

Transaction 1 (T1) updates Row 1 (R1). After that Transaction 2 (T2) updates Row 2 (R2). At the moment, there is an exclusive lock on R1 by T1 and on R2 by T2.

Next, T1 tries to update R2 but starts waiting as there is an exclusive lock. At the same time T2 tries to update R1 but he also waits as there is an exclusive lock.

In this scenario the deadlock has occurred. Oracle will detect deadlocks in the database and resolve them automatically by rolling back on of the transactions.

158: Explain how Oracle manages row locks.

Answer:

Inside a transaction when a row is modified, an exclusive lock is placed on that row. Placing an exclusive lock on a row means adding an entry for this row in the data block header. This record will point the transaction id of the transaction that placed the lock.

So we can say that every row level locks are stored in data block headers. There is no central lock manager to track row level locks in a database.

When another transaction tries to update the same row, he will check if the transaction recorded in the header is still active. If the transaction is active, he will wait until that transaction ends.

Chapter 14

Transactions

159: User A is running a long uncommitted transaction with several DML statements on table Z. User B queries table Z and doesn't see the changed data. After 30 minutes he gets the ORA-01555 error. What happened?

Answer:

The first time user B didn't get the error because there was still relevant information in the undo segments. He didn't see changed data, correctly, because user A's transaction was not committed. This is a feature of the read isolation committed level.

160: What is a transaction?

Answer:

A transaction is the smallest logical unit in a database. When you execute a DML statement in your session, you start a transaction implicitly. That transaction will last until you explicitly end it by executing a commit or rollback.

The reason why transaction is called the smallest unit is that, either all the changes made inside a transaction become permanent or all of the changes are rolled back. A transaction cannot be divided further into smaller parts.

Also Oracle assigns a unique id to each active transaction.

161: Give an example of a business process where using a transaction would be necessary.

Answer:

I'll give an example to transaction of a regular online sale example. Let's say you have an application where customers can make purchases online.

When the client chooses a product, enter all required information and finally click the buy button, these steps should happen in the database.

a) Drop the price of the product from client's account.

b) Add the price of the product to the seller's account.

c) Drop the amount of product by one in seller's stock.

When all these steps are performed, the selling will be successful. However all these steps are essential for the selling process to complete so we'll define these steps in a transaction. They will either complete altogether or they will completely fail.

162: List all the possibilities a transaction can end.

Answer:

a) The user executes a "commit" explicitly or the user executes "rollback" explicitly with a "savepoint" clause.

b) The user executes a DDL statement. This will implicitly end the transaction with a commit.

c) The server processes which was running the transaction crashes unexpectedly. In such a situation, the crash of the process will be detected by the PMON background instance process and the transaction will be rolled back implicitly.

d) Some Oracle tools (for ex: SQL*Plus) either commits or rolls back when you exit them. The behavior depends on the configuration of these applications.

163: What is the difference between the statement -level atomicity and transaction-level atomicity?

Answer:

A statement is a single SQL statement like UPDATE/DELETE/INSERT. A single statement is atomic by nature. It will either complete totally or all the changes will be rolled back. You don't have control over this mechanism. For example, you've execute an update statement which will update 80 rows. Either 80 rows will be updates or none of them.

In a transaction level atomicity, either all the statements in a transaction are committed or all of them are rolled back. You can create savepoints inside a transaction and rollback to that specific point if you want. You have control to some extent.

164: What can be advantage of naming a transaction?
Answer:

Transactions in an instance are identified by a transaction ID which is actually a pointer to the relevant undo segment that transaction uses. You can locate a transaction by its Transaction ID in v$transaction view.

However, that transaction id is not much user friendly. When you explicitly set a name to a transaction, you get a user friendly name for that transaction which makes it easy to track. You can easily recognize the transaction from its name.

This name is even written to online redo log records.

165: What is an "active" transaction and what is the effect of an active transaction on the database structures?
Answer:

An active transaction is a transaction which has started but not ended yet. It hasn't been committed or rolled back either explicitly or implicitly.

The active transaction will have exclusive locks on the rows that it has modified. There will be redo records for the changes it has made. It will also have undo records for the changes it has made. These undo records will be stored in undo segments. There will be data blocks in the SGA which were modified by this transaction. These blocks might also be flushed to disk if there is no free room in buffer cache but this doesn't mean that the changes have become permanent. They will become permanent if the transaction is committed.

166: What happens when a commit occurs for a transaction either explicitly or implicitly?

Answer:

A transaction starts when you issue the first DML statement. During a transaction you may execute multiple DML statements. These statements will change data blocks in buffer cache, will create redo records for the changes and will also create undo records for the changes.

The changed data blocks may even be flushed to disk but this doesn't mean that the changes have become permanent. They will only become permanent once you perform a commit.

When you execute a commit, a commit record is written to online redo log files. Oracle will halt the database until that commit record is stored on disk successfully.

As the transaction has ended, all the locks acquired during the transaction will be released. If a save point was declared in that transaction, it will be deleted as well.

167: What happens when a rollback occurs for a transaction either explicitly or implicitly?

Answer:

A transaction starts when you issue the first DML statement. During a transaction you may execute multiple DML statements. These statements will change data blocks in buffer cache, will create redo records for the changes and will also create undo records for the changes.

The changed data blocks may even be flushed to disk but this doesn't mean that the changes have become permanent. They will only become permanent once you perform a commit.

If a rollback occurs, all the changes made during that transaction will be reverted. Oracle will use relevant undo records to revert the data blocks. Also all the locks acquired during that transaction will be released. If a save point was declared in that transaction, it will be deleted as well.

168: What is an autonomous transaction?

Answer:

A transaction is atomic by nature. You can run multiple statements or call other routines inside a transaction. These will both succeed as a whole and become permanent or they will all be rolled back.

That's the normal implementation of transactions. However it is possible to define a routine as "autonomous" using the PRAGMA directive. If a stored program is defined as autonomous, it will run independent from the main transaction that called that routine.

The autonomous might commit or rollback but this won't affect the base transaction. The base transaction might go on and commit in the end even if the autonomous transaction rolls back. Or, changes committed in an autonomous transaction will be permanent even if the base transaction rolls back.

169: What is a distributed transaction?

Answer:

It is possible to link two or more databases using database links. With the help of a database link, you can reach the objects on a separate database inside the current database. For example in a SQL query you can reference both the objects in the current database and the objects in the remote database. This architecture is called distributed architecture.

In a distributed architecture, it is possible to start a transaction which will modify the data both in the current database and the remote database. A separate transaction will start on the remote database. If any error occurs in remote or local database, all the local and remote transactions will be rolled back. Such transactions are called distributed transactions.

This page is intentionally left blank.

Chapter 15

Storage Structures

170: You have one datafile in a mount point /opt. Due to application data growth, the datafile has maxed out the available space. You want to reduce the size of the datafile. The application team, deletes a huge table of historical data. Was this enough?

Answer:

No. Deleting just data does not change the datafile size. You need to do a manual resize of the datafile, up to the point where there is no more data beyond it. If needed some extents or segments will need to be moved to a point below (with move and shrink commands).

171: What are the physical structures of an Oracle Database?

Answer:

There are three types of data files in an Oracle database. These are data files, control files and online redo log files. The data files can also be categorized as "data files", "temporary files". The data files hold regular data and the temporary data files hold temporary data required by users.

The control file holds the metadata of the database and is an essential part of the database. It stores the physical location of database files.

The online redo log files holds the change vectors made to data files. These change records contain the changes to undo table spaces as well.

172: Where can you store a database file? What are the alternatives?

Answer:

The recommended way to store a data files is to use Automatic Storage Management (ASM). ASM is Oracle's own disk and volume manager. In ASM, Oracle manages the raw disks itself without the need for a file system.

You can also store the database files on a regular file system like ext3, ext4 on Linux or NTFS on Windows. These are regular file system which you can also store non-database related files.

For Real Application Clusters (RAC), you can store the database files in a cluster file system. The cluster file system should be certified by Oracle.

The last option is to use raw disks. The raw disks allow you to perform direct i/o to underlying disks but this option is not common today. ASM is the recommended way.

173: What are the advantages of using ASM (Automatic Storage Management) over a regular file system?

Answer:

When you use ASM, you can make direct I/O to the underlying disks. If you use a file system, there will be an overhead of using the file system. You have to use the interfaces of that file system.

The maintenance is easier in ASM. ASM will manage the disks itself. In a file system you need to manage the disks yourself. ASM acts like a volume manager. You can dynamically add disks to it or remove disks from it. Regular file systems don't have these capabilities. You have to use a separate volume manager.

ASM distributes the files to each underlying disks and because of that it provides a better I/O performance.

174: What is the relationship between an ASM disk and an ASM disk group?

Answer:

An ASM disk corresponds to a physical disk that is known by the operating system. The disk will have a device file associated with it. When you make a regular disk and "ASM Disk", Oracle writes metadata to the disk's header and that disk becomes part of ASM.

An ASM disk group is a group of related ASM Disks. ASM disk group is a logical term. One or more ASM disks form an ASM disk group. Each database file can belong only to a single

ASM disk group. ASM instance distributes the file extents evenly to the ASM disks in an ASM disk group.

175: Explain the relationship between an ASM extent, ASM Allocation Unit, ASM file and ASM Disk Group.

Answer:

An ASM allocation unit (AU) is the smallest unit of storage area allocated in an ASM disk group by Oracle. The size of the allocation unit is determined at creation of the disk group.

ASM instance, divides an ASM file into ASM extents. An ASM extent is the minimum storage area allocated for an ASM file. Multiple Allocation Units can form an ASM extent and multiple ASM extents can form an ASM file.

ASM files reside in ASM disk groups. A file can reside only in a single ASM disk group but the extents of that file will be distributed among the disks in that disk group evenly.

176: What is an ASM instance? How does it work?

Answer:

The structure of an ASM instance resembles database instances. It is composed of background processes and shared area.

An ASM instance is responsible for managing the ASM disks, ASM disk groups, ASM files, file extents and allocation units.

An ASM instance works in collaboration with database instances. When a database instance or a server process wants to access a file stored in an ASM instance, it asks the location of the file to the ASM instance. ASM instance provides the location of the requested file but does not touch the file. It is still the server process or the database instance processes which modify the files stored in ASM.

177: Explain how data is organized physically inside database?

Answer:

The smallest unit that can be allocated for storage of data files is database block. The default database block is 8K in size. The minimum operation that Oracle can perform will be on data blocks.

The data blocks form extents which are continuous data blocks. The size of extents can be uniform or dynamic according to the options you've set during creation.

Externs form the data files. An extent can reside only in a database. It cannot span multiple data files. Data files are the biggest physical structure in database storage.

178: Explain how data is organized logically inside database?

Answer:

The smallest unit that can be allocated for storage of data files is database block. Data blocks are physical structures and they form extents. Extents are continuous data blocks and they are physical too.

Extents form segments. A segment is a logical term. Any schema object that contains data has a segment. Tables, indexes, materialized views etc. are all examples of segment.

An extent cannot span multiple data files but a segment can span multiple data files.

A segment can reside only in one tablespace. A tablespace is a logical structure and it corresponds to a group of related data files.

179: At what points does a temporary data file differ from a permanent data file?
Answer:
a) Temp files work in NOLOGGING mode. Redo logs are not generated for changes made in a temp file and during recovery, the temp files are skipped.
b) You can make a permanent file read-only but it is not possible to make a temp file read-only.
c) You can create permanent files with ALTER DATABASE command but it is not possible to do the same for temp files.
d) The temp files are not listed in "v$datafile" view, they are listed in "v$tempfile" view.

180: When are temporary tablespaces used?
Answer:
Every user needs a permanent tablespace and a temporary tablespace to hold data. There will be a default permanent tablespace and a default temporary tablespace in the database. It is also possible to assign each user its own default permanent and temporary tablespaces.

The temporary tablespaces store objects and data whose life time is user session. When you create temporary tables, these objects are stored in temporary tablespaces.

Also, server processes may use temporary tablespace during certain activities like sort and hash operations, if the memory reserved for that server process (PGA) is not enough.

Again the results returned from a query may be kept in temporary tablespaces if the memory is not sufficient.

181: What are the statuses of data files?

Answer:

Most of the time we expect the data files to be online, which means the data file is available and you can read from it or write to it.

You can make a data file read-only by making its tablespace read-only. You can only read from a read-only data file. You cannot write to it or update it.

It is also possible to make a data file offline. If a data file is offline, you cannot access it either for reading or writing. It will be inaccessible. It is possible to make a data file offline, and leave the tablespace online or you can make the entire tablespace offline. A datafile will also be taken offline automatically if Oracle cannot access it.

182: What kind of information is stored in a control file?

Answer:

The control file stores structural information about a database.

For example it contains the path of the online redolog files, data files and archive log files.

The metadata of the backup files are also stored in control file. You can also use a catalog server at the same time to store these metadata.

Every database is assigned a unique Database ID (DBID). This DBID is stored in control file.

Every change made to a database is assigned a System Check Number (SCN). The SCAN at the time of check points are also recorded in the control file.

183: Explain the control file importance for a database and how it can be protected.

Answer:

A control file is one of the most critical parts of an Oracle database. It holds information about the structure of the database like path of online redolog files, data files and archive log files. It holds all the information to open a database. Without a control file, Oracle database cannot run. Even a running instance will shut down if a control file goes missing. Because of this, it is important to protect the control files. You have the ability to maintain multiple identical copies the control files. Storing a copy on different storage hardware will provide fault tolerance against hardware failures.

184: How do online redo log files work?

Answer:

Online redo log files holds change records. When a change is made to a data file in the database, the change is also recorded in online redo log files. There will be multiple online redolog groups in a database. These groups work in a circular fashion. When one of the groups is filled, Oracle will start writing to next group.

When all the groups are filled, Oracle will return to the first group and start writing there.

A separate process called LGWR (Log Writer) is responsible for writing redo records to online redo log files.

185: Explain what happens when a user updates a record in the database.

Answer:

First, that block is read from the disk into the buffer cache if it is not already there. The change is written to the online redo log buffer. When a commit occurs inside the transaction, a commit record is also written to the online redolog files. A commit guarantees that all the records in the log buffer is written to online redo log files.

After the redo record is written, the data block in the database buffer cache is updated. The block is not immediately written to the data files stored on disk. It will be written later when a check point occurs or when database buffer cache runs low on free space.

186: How can we protect our online redo log files?

Answer:

Changes made to data blocks in a database are first written to online redo log files. Commit records which guarantee that the changes will be permanent is also written to online redolog files and they are used during recovery. Therefore you need to protect your online redolog files. Loss of that file will lead to data loss.

The best way to protect online redolog files is to multiplex them. A redo log group can have identical multiple copies. These copies are called member. If you place the members on different storage hardware, you can protect your online redolog files against hardware failures.

187: What is archived log file and why are they used?

Answer:

Online redolog files are used in a circular fashion. The log writer process (lgwr) starts from the first group and when that group is filled up, it advances to the next group. When all the groups are filled, the log write returns to the beginning and starts overwriting the first redo log group.

If database is working in "noarchivelog" mode, you'll have lost the changes when an online redolog file is overwritten. If the database is working in archivelog mode, the online redolog file will be copied to a separate location when it is filled up. These files are called archive log files and they can be used to recover database.

188: Explain the relationship between a database data block and an operating system block.

Answer:

A database block is the smallest unit of database that can be allocated in an Oracle database. The minimum data operation in a database will be to a data block. The default data block size is 8K in Oracle.

Similarly, an operating system block is the smallest unit you can allocate on the file system where you create a file. The operating system block size is file system dependent. The default block size in an ext3 file system is 4K.

If you use the default block sizes, a data block (8K) operation in the database will be performed with two operations at operating system level (4K).

189: How can ROWID be used to locate a row?

Answer:

There are three pieces of information stored in a ROWID that you can use to locate row. File number, block number and row number is stored in ROWID in a special format. The rowid can be deciphered into file number, block number and row number.

The file number is the file id of the data file that stores the row. Every data file in a database is given a unique ID.

The block number is the number of the block inside that data file. Each data block has a unique number inside a data file. And finally row number is the number of the row inside the data block.

190: Explain what "Row Chaining" and "Row Migration" means.

Answer:

Every data block has a certain size. Data blocks contain rows. If the length of a row does not fit into a single data block, it can span multiple data blocks. In such a situation, a pointer is inserted at the end of the block which points to the next data block at which the row continues. This is called "row chaining". The blocks of a row are chained.

Sometimes a row can fit into a single data block. Later, the row can be updated and its length may increase. However, the new length may not fit into the data block. In such a situation, the contents of the row are copied to a new data block and a pointer is created on the original data block.

191: Why do we need undo segments in an Oracle database?

Answer:

Undo tablespaces hold before-images of changed data. When a data block is changed, the change record is written to online redo log files and the initial version of the change is written to the relevant undo segment in the undo tablespace.

This undo data can be used to rollback changes made inside a transaction. You can revert the changes made with undo records.

The same undo records are also used for consistent reading. In a consistent read, the data block might have changed while a query is running but the query will show you the block as if it has never changed. This is done using undo blocks and consistent reading is Oracle's default behavior.

192: What is High Water Mark (HWM)?
Answer:

When data is inserted into a table, Oracle will allocate new extents to hold the rows. This is the default behavior. The table will keep extending as long as new data comes. Later, some data may be deleted from the table. There will be sparse free space in such a situation. Later when you insert new data, Oracle will use this free space instead of allocating new space. The furthest point the table has reached by allocating new space is called High Water Mark (HWM). The HWM has a special part in database processes. For example, when doing a full table scan, Oracle will read all the data up to the HWM.

193: What are the default tablespaces found in an Oracle database?
Answer:

There are standard tablespaces which you can find in an Oracle database. These are:

a) **SYSTEM Tablespace**: This tablespace holds the data dictionary which is required for Oracle database to operate.

b) **SYSAUX Tablespace**: This tablespace does not hold

system data but is required by Oracle database features to operate. For example: Automatic Workload Repository.

c) **UNDO Tablespace**: This tablespace holds undo segments which is filled during transactions.

d) **TEMP Tablespace**: This tablespace is used for storing temporary objects.

e) **USERS Tablespace**: Every database needs a default permanent tablespace to hold user data. USERS tablespace will be the default tablespace of the database.

194: What is undo retention in an Oracle database?
Answer:

Undo records are primarily used for consistent reads and rollback operations. They are an essential part of the database. Undo records produced during a transaction are stored in undo tablespaces.

The size of an undo tablespace is limited so there can be only a limited undo records in a database. When you set undo retention, you set the time limit for how long undo records will be kept. This is set using the UNDO_RETENTION instance parameter. The value shows the undo retention period in seconds.

Chapter 16

Oracle Instance Architecture

195: If you have a Data Guard configuration with one primary and one standby, and the standby for network reasons lags beyond the available archives on the primary, how do you fix the issue?

Answer:

You can retrieve the archivelogs manually from the backups and apply them to the standby until the gap closes. If this isn't possible or there are too many archives, you can rebuild the environment by backing up the primary and using the backup to recreate the standby.

196: You have a 3 node Oracle RAC. A user creates 3 different connections from 3 different clients (for example: sqlplus, sqldeveloper and excel) on the same machine. Do all these connections go to the same node?

Answer:

Only if you connect directly to a specific instance, using the instance name in your connection URL. If, following good practices, you include all the nodes in your tnsnames entry / url, the different connections will be balanced between all the nodes, possibly landing on the same node or not.

197: Can you have ASM configured with RAC? What are the benefits of having ASM configured?

Answer:

Yes you can. They are complementing technologies. ASM provides a storage abstraction level by grouping several disks into one Diskgroup. This simplifies the space administration and allows the creation of failover and mirrored groups, increasing DB reliability.

198: What are the differences between single instance architecture and RAC architecture?

Answer:

In single instance architecture, there will be a single database and a single instance.

In a RAC environment, again there will be a single database but there will be multiple instances. These instances will share the same data and will be a part of the same database.

In RAC architecture, if the database name is ORCL then the instances will be named ORCL1, ORCL2, ORCL3... respectively. In single instance architecture we expect the name of the instance to be equal to the database name.

In single instance architecture, the database will run on a single machine but in RAC the database will be composed of several machines.

199: At what stages does an instance pass respectively while starting up ?

Answer:

An instance is initially "shutdown" which means there is no process or memory area allocated for it. When you execute the "startup" command, the instance first starts up. Now the instance is in "nomount" stage. At this stage the instance is started, the background processes are created and shared memory is allocated.

Then the instance moves to "mount" stage where the control file is read and the instance is associated with the database. After that, the data files and online redo log files are read and the database is opened. At this stage the database is "open".

200: With what privileges can you connect to an instance?

Answer:

To connect to an instance, the minimum required privilege is "CREATE SESSION" system privilege. There is also a role named "CONNECT" which grants the "CREATE SESSION" privilege. These privileges will connect you to the instance as a regular user.

The connecting user may have "SYSDBA" privileges which is

the most powerful privilege in the database. Users with that privilege can do anything.

There is another privilege named "SYSOPER" which can be used for operator tasks. The SYSDBA and SYSOPER privileges also let you connect to a database which is in shutdown state.

201: How does Oracle start an instance?

Answer:

You can start the instance by connecting to a down database with SQL*Plus and then execute "STARTUP" command or you can use SRVCTL tool to do the same thing.

The first thing Oracle does is to locate the server parameter file. It can either find an spfile or a text based parameter file. It reads the parameters which determine the characteristic of the instance.

The system global area (SGA) is allocated in the memory. The instance background parameters are also started.

At this stage, the alert file of the instance is also opened and Oracle writes the explicitly set parameters to this file.

202: What does mounting a database mean and what operations can be performed on the database while it is in a mount state?

Answer:

Before an instance moves to a mount state, it will be in "nomount" state. In "nomount" state, the instance is started, background processes are created and memory is allocated.

When the database moves to mount state, the control file is located and read. The control file has to exist. The location of the control file is specified in "CONTROL_FILES" instance parameter.

In mount state, the instance is associated with a database. The paths of the files forming the database are read but their existence is not verified. They will be verified when the database is opened.

At mount state, normal users cannot connect to the database but administrators can and they can perform administrative tasks.

203: How is a database opened after the mount stage?

Answer:

At mount stage, Oracle retrieves the path of the files required for opening a file but it doesn't check whether these files really exists.

While opening a database, Oracle locates all the data files except the undo tablespace in the database. It then opens an undo tablespace. The undo tablespace to open is acquired from the UNDO_TABLESPACE initialization parameter.

Finally the online redo log files are opened and the database becomes available for access to regular users.

204: At what stages does an open Oracle instance pass until it is shut down?

Answer:

To shut down an open database, you need to issue the "shutdown" command from SQL*Plus or you need to use SRVCTL command line tool.

The database will first move to "mount" state. At this state, the database will only be available to administrators. Regular users won't be able to make connection. The database will be closed. But the control file will still be open.

Next, the database will move to "nomount" state. The control file will also be closed. Only the instance will be up.

The final state is the "shutdown" state where the instance will also be terminated. The memory allocated for instance will be released and the background processes will be killed.

205: Explain what happens during a checkpoint and why is it needed?

Answer:

A checkpoint is a critical mechanism in Oracle. When a checkpoint occurs, Oracle writes the dirty buffers in the db block buffer cache to the data files on the disk. It also writes the System Change Number (SCN) to control files and data files headers. The SCN is recorded as the checkpoint change number.

A checkpoint ensures that the db is consistent up to that SCN number because all the changes up that time have been written to disk. It is used in recovery operations.

206: What happens during instance recovery?

Answer:

While opening an instance, if Oracle detects that an instance recovery is needed, it will first apply all redo records it by beginning from the time of the instance failure. It will apply all the changes whether they were committed or not. This is called "roll forward" phase. At this phase, the undo segments will also be populated.

When applying the changes finishes, Oracle will roll back all the changes made at the transactions which did not commit before the instance failure. This phase is called "roll back" phase.

207: When does an instance recovery occur? How do you start it?

Answer:

First of all, an instance recovery starts automatically when required. You cannot start it manually with a command or other means.

An instance recovery occurs while you open a database. If you have performed a "clean" shutdown, then while opening a database no instance recovery will occur. The data files, control file and online redo log files will be consistent.

However, if you have shut down the instance with "shutdown abort" or the instance crashed because of an exception then an instance recovery will occurs while you try to open the database. It will be required to carry the database to a consistent state.

208: What kind of messages can be found in an alert log file?
Answer:
There will be one alert file for each database instance. You can find messages regarding critical errors occurred in the instance. For example all internal errors (ora-600 errors) can be seen in the log file. Deadlocks are also reported in the alert log file. While an instance is started, initialization parameters which were set explicitly are spooled to the alert log file.

If you are using shared server architecture, you can messages relating to shared servers and dispatchers.

If an error occurs while a materialized view is being refreshed automatically, this is also reported in the log file.

209: What are the basic memory structures found in an Oracle instance?
Answer:
a) **System Global Area (SGA):** This area is a shared memory and it is accessible by all server processes. The data, whose scope is instance, is stored in this area. It is allocated while an instance starts.

b) **Program Global Area (PGA):** This area is specific to each server process and is only accessible by that server process. It is allocated when a server process starts and is released when the process dies.

c) **User Global Area (UGA):** This area is specific to a

database session.

d) **Software Code**: This is a special area where the running code of the Oracle software resides.

210: What are the options of managing Oracle instance memory?

Answer:

There are three options to manage memory for an Oracle instance.

a) **Automatic Memory Management**: In this mode, you set the amount of memory that will be used for both System Global Area (SGA) and Program Global Area (PGA). Oracle regulates the percentage of memory that will be allocated for SGA and PGA separately.

b) **Automatic Shared Memory** Management: In this mode, you set the amount of memory that will be used by SGA and PGA separately. Oracle manages how much memory will be allocated to each sub section in SGA separately.

c) **Manual Memory Management**: In this mode, you explicitly set the amount of memory that will be used by each section of SGA separately.

211: What are the parts of Program Global Area (PGA)?

Answer:

Program Global Area (PGA) is composed of sub-parts.

a) **SQL Work Areas**: This area is used by certain SQL

operations by the server process. There are three memory areas for in the SQL work areas. These are: "Hash Area", "Sort Area" and "Bitmap Merge Area".

b) **Session Memory**: This area holds session specific data.

c) **Private SQL Area**: This section has also two parts: "Persistent Area" and "Runtime Area". The private SQL area holds primarily stores data related to execution of SQL queries. For ex: bind variables.

212: What is the role of database buffer cache?

Answer:

Database buffer cache is part of System Global Area (SGA). The buffer cache holds the data blocks in RAM. The data blocks are normally part of data files stored on disk.

When a data block will be updated, it is first read from the disk into the db buffer cache and then updated there.

Again for read operations, the data block first is read into the db buffer cache.

If the sought data block is already in the cache, then no disk I/O is performed. This improves performance because memory I/O is much more faster than disk I/O. The buffer cache minimizes the disk I/O.

213: What are the states of buffers in database buffer cache?

Answer:

The database block buffers can be found in three states.

a) **Unused**: These buffers are never used before.

b) **Dirty**: These buffers were read from the data files stored on disk. They were updated by SQL queries but they have not been written to the disk yet. The data block on the disk and the block on the buffer is not same. This is why they are called dirty buffers.

c) **Clean**: The data block on the disk and the block on the cache is same. They are not "dirty".

214: When are the dirty blocks written to disk?

Answer:

SQL queries may update data. When a data block will be updated, Oracle first searches the db buffer cache. If it cannot find the block there, it reads the data block from the disk into buffer cache and updates the block there. That block becomes "dirty".

When a checkpoint occurs, Oracle writes the dirty buffers in the cache to disk. After a checkpoint the data block on the disk and the data block in the buffer are synchronized.

Sometimes, the db buffer cache might be full. There might not be room for new data blocks. In this case, Oracle will also write dirty buffers to disk to release some space.

215: What is "current mode get" and "consistent read get"?

Answer:

In a "current mode get" Oracle retrieves the data block exactly as it resides on the db buffer cache. It doesn't modify it. This usually happens for update operations.

In a "consistent read get", Oracle modifies a copy of the data block in the buffer with undo data to revert it to a point in time. The copy of the block is modified on memory. This usually happens due to the SELECT queries because Oracle has to show you the results when a SELECT query began.

216: What is the use of redo log buffer inside System Global Area (SGA)?
Answer:
The redo log buffer cache is a separate area in System Global Area (SGA). Its size is determined by the LOG_BUFFER initialization parameter. The area is a fixed size area. It is not managed dynamically.

When a data block is changed inside database, a redo record is created for this change. This change record is first written to the redo log buffer before the change is actually applied to the data block. This mechanism provides ability to recover changes in case of a failure.

The change records in the redo log buffer are written to the online redo log buffers on disk sequentially.

217: Explain the structure of the Shared Pool inside SGA?
Answer:
Shared Pool inside the System Global Area is a sub-component of SGA. It has also its own sub-components. Almost any operation performed in an instance interacts with the shared pool. The main sub-components of the shared pool is as

follows:

a) **Library Cache**: The parsed SQL statements and execution plans for the SQL queries are stored in this area. This is the biggest part of shared pool. It has its own sub-components also. They are "Shared SQL Area" and "Private SQL Area".

b) **Data Dictionary Cache**: Oracle refers to the data dictionary frequently while running so the content of the data dictionary is cached in this area. The size of this area is fixed.

c) **Server Result Cache**: The SQL query result cache and PL/SQL function result cache is stored in this area.

218: What is the difference between a "soft parse" and a "hard parse"?

Answer:

When a user submits an SQL query, that SQL query is first parsed by the server process. An execution plan has to be prepared for that query. An execution plan determines how Oracle will retrieve the result that is requested in the query. There may be multiple paths that will lead to the same result. The optimizer engine will try to find the one with the lowest cost.

Preparing the execution plans has an overhead. To improve performance, Oracle caches the execution plans inside library cache. When an SQL query is submitted, if the execution plan is found in the library cache, that plan is used. This is called a "soft parse". If no execution plan is found in the library cache, Oracle prepares one from scratch. This is called a "hard parse".

219: What would you do to minimize the hard parses?
Answer:

The first time an SQL query is submitted to database for execution, Oracle prepares an execution plan from scratch. This is called a "hard parse". This execution plan is cached in library cache. If later, the same SQL query is submitted, Oracle uses the execution plan in the cache. This is called a "soft parse". As preparing an execution plan has an overhead, you'd like to minimize it.

The most important thing to prevent hard parses is to execute parametric queries. Because, for Oracle to do a soft parse, the SQL text has to be identical. Different values in the WHERE clauses will force a hard parse.

Also you need to send exactly the same text from the clients. Even the case of the text will cause a hard parse.

220: What is Large Pool and where is it used?
Answer:

Large Pool is a sub-component inside System Global Area (SGA). This memory area is optional. If defined, it is used for large operations like RMAN backups. If you do not define it, the shared pool will be used. Large operations might quickly fill the shared pool which will affect the performance of other operations going on in the database. It is better to use a separate area for such operations.

Also in a shared server architecture, the user global area (UGA) will also be allocated inside large pool.

221: Explain the "Software Code Area" memory areas.

Answer:

Software Code Area is a special area in memory where the code for the Oracle Database software is stored. This area is a protected area and it is more exclusive than other areas.

You install Oracle software on disk. The binary files are stored on disk but when they are going to be executed, they are loaded into memory.

The size of this area is fixed. It is not managed dynamically. The amount of memory that will be reserved for this area is platform specific. Also when you install a new version of the software, the amount of the memory allocated might change.

222: What are the main types of processes you can find in an Oracle environment?

Answer:

You can find three main types of processes in an Oracle environment. These are:

a) **Client Processes**: These run on the client. Clients are usually run on separate machines but it is also possible to run client processes on the same server with the database. Clients make connection to the database.

b) **Background Processes**: These belong to instance. When

the instance starts up they are created and they are
killed when the instance terminates. These processes
perform the tasks that an instance has to carry on.

c) **Server Processes**: These are created per client connected
to the database. They execute the SQL queries
submitted by users and return result to the clients.

223: What is the difference between "dedicated server architecture" and "shared server architecture"?

Answer:

In dedicated server architecture, a separate server process is
created for each session. The SQL queries submitted by that
user are executed by that server process and again the result is
returned by that server process to the client.

In shared server architecture, the server processes are shared
by sessions. One shared server can service multiple users. The
"dispatcher" processes communicate with user processes. They
carry the request to shared server processes, the shared server
processes execute the command, deliver the results to
dispatchers and finally the dispatchers return the results back
to clients.

224: What is the duty of the SMON background process?

Answer:

SMON stands for system monitor. SMON is responsible for
clean-up operations at system level.

The main duty of SMON is to perform instance recovery.

Instance recovery occurs at startup of the instance automatically if required. If the database was shutdown "cleanly" then the all the database files will be consistent and no instance recovery will occur. However, if the database was shutdown with "abort" option or if the instance crashed due to an error then the database files will be inconsistent and an instance recovery will be performed by SMON at startup.

225: When does the log writer process write redo records from the buffer to disk?

Answer:

The redo log buffer cache is a memory area inside the system global area (SGA). The log writer process (LGWR) is responsible writing the contents of the buffer to the online redo log files that are stored on disk.

The write operation occurs when user performs a commit inside a transaction. The write operation will happen in every 3 seconds even if no activity occurs.

A logfile switch will also force writing. If the 1/3 of the buffer gets full or 1MB of redo record is collected in the buffer again the contents are written to the online redo log files.

226: Why is it a bad idea at performance perspective to commit too frequently?

Answer:

Changes made by a server process is first written to the redo log buffer as a change record and later the change is actually applied to data block in database buffer cache. When user submits a commit command inside a transaction, a commit record with the current system change number (SCN) at that moment is written to redo log buffer.

The commit forces the contents of the redo log buffer to be written to disk.

According to the rules of Oracle database management system, a commit command should make sure that changes made inside the transaction become permanent. To guarantee that the commit has succeeded, Oracle will halt the system until it writes the redo records to online redo log files on disk. If you perform too frequent commits, the halt steps will degrade the performance.

227: What is the role of "checkpoint" process in an instance?
Answer:
The name of the checkpoint process is "ckpt" at operating system level.

Checkpoint is an important mechanism in Oracle. It is used in recovery operations. When a checkpoint occurs, all the dirty buffers in the database buffer cache is written to disk and the control files and data file headers are updated with the SCN at the time of checkpoint.

When the time for a checkpoint comes, the ckpt process updates the control files and data file headers with the current SCN. It also signals database writer process and the DBWN process writes the dirty buffers to disk.

228: What are the most common three types of checkpoints?

Answer:

There are three types of checkpoints.

a) **Thread Checkpoint:** These checkpoints are applied by a redo in a thread. If all the threads take place this is called a database thread.

b) **Datafile and Tablespace Checkpoints:** These checkpoints occur only for the datafiles in a tablespace. They do not cover the whole database. For example, if you take a tablespace read-only or offline, a tablespace check point occurs.

c) **Incremental Checkpoints:** In incremental checkpoints, the data is not fully written. It is partially written to avoid writing large data chunks.

229: When do thread checkpoints occur?

Answer:

There are four events where a thread checkpoint occurs. These are:

a) When you shut down a database consistently. For example when you shutdown with immediate option.

b) When you explicitly execute "alter system checkpoint" command. This command forces a manual checkpoint.

c) When an online redo log file switch occurs. A thread checkpoint is the result of a log file switch. However the reason for a log file switch is different.

d) When you put the database in backup mode with "alter

database begin backup" command. This command is
used in user-managed backups.

230: What are the two types of instance parameter s?
Answer:

The instance parameters are also called initialization
parameters as they are used to control how an instance starts
up and operates. We can divide them into two main groups.
The basic initialization parameters and advanced parameters.
There are nearly thirty parameters that belong to basic group.
They define basic characteristic of a database like name of the
database, physical location of data files, database block size.
They should be sufficient enough to run a database under
normal circumstances. The advanced parameters are required
for certain situations where advanced tuning is necessary.

231: What is the difference between a text based parameter file and server parameter file?
Answer:

The text-based parameter files are called pfile (parameter file).
A pfile is a plain text file. You can open it with a text editor and
change the parameters. However, you need to restart the
instance for changes to take effect. You cannot change the run-
time values on the fly.

A server parameter file is a binary file. You cannot open it with
a text editor and change parameters. You need to change the
parameters with "ALTER SYSTEM" command. However, the

dynamic parameters can be changed while the instance is running. You don't have to restart the instance.

232: Explain the directory structure of Automatic Diagnostic Repository.

Answer:

The Automatic Diagnostic Repository (ADR) is a file based repository for keeping diagnostic files. It has a certain directory structure.

At the top, there is ADR base and this path is determined by "diagnostic_dest" instance parameter. The first directory is "diag" directory. According to the products installed on the server, you find a separate directory under "diag" like "lsnrctl", "tnslsnr" , "rdbms" etc. The "rdbms" directory holds files for databases. The structure goes like this:

rdbms\<database_name>\<instance_name>\

For Real Application systems, the database name and the instance name will be different.

233: What are the main directories and files found in Automatic Diagnostic Repository (ADR) for an RDBMS?

Answer:

The RDBMS directory holds diagnostic files for databases running on that server. The main structure is

"rdbms\<database_name>\<instance_name>\"

Under the <instance_name> directory, the main directories are:

a) **alert:** This directory holds a file named "log.xml" which has the same content with "alert.log" file but it keeps them in XML format so you can programmatically access them.

b) **cdump:** This directory holds the core dump files.

c) **trace:** This is the most used directory. It holds the main diagnostic file (alert.log) file and other trace files (.trc files) created for background and server processes.

234: What kind of messages is stored in "alert.log" file?

Answer:

The "alert.log" file is a text file, which is found in ADR (Automatic Diagnostic Repository). It is the main diagnostic file to debug an instance. Instance related critic errors are logged in this directory. These critic errors can be internal error which start with ora-600, database block corruptions or deadlock errors.

The start or shut down operations are logged in this file as well. During startup, all non-default parameters are spooled. Errors related to shared server or dispatcher's processes are also spooled to this file as they are closely related with the instance's health.

Chapter 17

Oracle Database Memory Structures

235: When a new query is issued on the database an execution plan is generated. Is this before or after parsing and in which structure of the database are the execution plans stored?

Answer:

Execution plans are generated after parsing, phase that checks the syntax of the query and checks the relevant objects. The execution plan is then stored in the Shared SQL Area, belonging to the Library Cache, which is part of the Shared Pool, component of the SGA.

236: What are the characteristics of Shared Global Area (SGA)?

Answer:

Shared Global Area is a memory region in an Oracle instance.

As the name implies, it is a shared region area in the memory (RAM) of the server. It is accessible by all the processes (background + server processes). They keep data which is useful instance wide like database buffer cache, library cache data dictionary cache etc.

SGA is created when an instance starts and is removed from the memory when the instance terminates. The size of the SGA is adjustable. Several instance parameters determine its size and it is managed by the DBA.

237: What are the characteristics of Program Global Area (PGA)?

Answer:

Program Global Area (PGA) is a memory region in an Oracle instance. Unlike shared global area (SGA) it is not shared. It is exclusive to each server process or background process. That area cannot be accessed by another process.

A PGA can extend and shrink during the life time of the process which has created it. However, the DBA has the control on how much memory area will be allocated for all the PGAs. DBA can also control how much memory each sub component (SQL Work Areas, Private SQL Area, Session Memory etc.) will allocate.

A PGA area will be released when the process which has created dies.

238: What are the options of managing the memory of an instance?

Answer:

The most common used option is to use Automatic Memory Management. In Automatic memory management, you determine the total memory size that an instance will allocate in the server. Oracle determines how much memory each sub component will have. The management is dynamic. How much memory a sub component is adjusted (expand or shrink) at run-time.

On contrary, you can use manual memory management. In manual memory management, you explicitly specify how much memory each sub component will allocate. This is a more advanced technique. You should use Automatic Memory Management unless you are sure what you do.

239: What are the two different options when using Automatic Memory Management?

Answer:

The general idea behind Automatic Memory Management (AMM) is that a database administrator only determines the size of the total memory that will be allocated for the memory structures. You do not determine how much memory each sub component will use.

The AMM also has two options. "Automatic Memory Management" and "Automatic Shared Memory Management". In the first option, you set the total memory that Program

Global Area (PGA) and Shared Global Area (SGA) will allocate together. In the latter, you set how much memory PGA and SGA will allocate separately.

240: What is User Global Area (UGA) and how it behaves differently in Shared Server Architecture and Dedicated Server Architecture?
Answer:

User Global Area (UGA) is a memory region where session variables and session state is stored. If you're using dedicated server architecture, the User Global Area will be stored in Program Global Area (PGA) and that session variables will be specific to that server process.

However, when using shared server architecture, the user global area will be kept in Shared Global Area (SGA). The UGA has to be kept in a shared location as there will be no exclusive process for that session.

241: Describe what Private SQL Area is.
Answer:

The Private SQL Area is a memory region which is a part of Program Global Area (PGA). The private SQL area is also divided into two regions. The Persistent Area and the Run Time Area.

The persistent area remains as long as the session remains. It holds the bind variables which are attached to SQL queries. The runtime area stores the state information of query executions. For each cursor, a private SQL area is allocated. The number of cursors (so the number of private SQL areas) is determined by the "OPEN_CURSORS" instance parameter.

242: Describe what SQL Work Areas are.
Answer:

SQL work areas are memory regions in Program Global Area (PGA). They are used when the server process needs memory area for certain operations. For example a "sort area" is an SQL work area where rows returned from a query is sorted. Similarly a "hash area" when the server process performs a hash join operation.

The sizes of these areas are determined automatically by Oracle when you use automatic memory management. In manual memory management you have to explicitly set the size of each SQL work area.

If the size of an SQL work area cannot fulfill an operation, the server process may use temporary area on disk. This will slow down the response.

243: Why is a mechanism like "database buffer cache" needed in an Oracle Instance?
Answer:

The disk I/O is an expensive operation in terms of response time. The disk technology depends on platters and spinning disks. However the memory access is much more faster. If we can store the data we want in memory (RAM) then the response time will dramatically increase. The problem is that, the RAM is volatile and it is expensive. We cannot store everything we want on RAM. The optimum solution is to store the most used data on RAM and to store less used data on disk. The database buffer cache just does this. The mechanism stores frequently accessed data blocks on RAM so that the accesses to these blocks are fast.

244: What are the three types of data block buffer states?
Answer:
A data block in database buffer cache can be in three states. These are:

a) **Unused:** This block has been created during buffer cache initiation but has never been used.

b) **Dirty:** A data block was read from disk into the cache and it was updated by a server process. The block on the cache is different from the corresponding block on the disk.

c) **Clean:** The data block in the buffer cache is the same as the corresponding data block on the disk.

245: What are the two buffer mode gets?
Answer:
There are two buffer mode gets - Current mode and consistent mode.

a) **Current Mode:** In this mode the most recent version of the block in the cache is read. For example let's say a block has been read into the cache and updated. It is now dirty. If we read this dirty block to modify again, this will be a current mode get. We get the block without touching it. Current mode is common during DML operations.

b) **Consistent Get:** When you start a read operation, Oracle returns you the version of the block at the time you started the select operation. This is called consistent get.

246: What is the difference between a physical read and logical read?

Answer:

The database blocks are not directly read from the datafiles stored on disk. When Oracle wants to read a data block which is not in the buffer cache, it first copies that block to buffer cache. This is the regular mechanism.

When Oracle has to read a data block it will first search the database buffer cache. This is called a **logical read** and default behavior as accessing RAM is much faster than disk access. If the sought data block doesn't reside in the cache, Oracle will retrieve the block from the disk. This is called a **physical read**.

247: What are the three types of buffer pools in database buffer cache?

Answer:

There are three types of buffer pools in database buffer cache.

a) **Default Buffer Pool:** This is the default buffer pool where the data blocks are cached.

b) **Recycle Pool:** Objects that are explicitly targeted for removal because of infrequent access are placed in this pool.

c) **Keep Pool:** Objects that are explicitly targeted to remain in the buffer cache are put into this pool.

The recycle pool and keep pool has to be explicitly enabled. The default buffer is created as a default.

248: What is redolog buffer used for?

Answer:

Before a change will be made to a data block, a record defining the change is first written to online redo log files and then the change is actually applied to the data block. This change record is called a redo log record. Again this redo record is not directly written to the online redo log files that are stored on disk. They are written to redo log buffer in the Shared Global Area. This specific memory region is called redo log buffer. Its size is static and it is created while instance starts.

249: What are the sub-components of shared pool? Explain them briefly.

Answer:

a) **Library Cache:** This is the largest part of the shared pool. It contains SQL and PL/SQL code. The execution plans for SQL queries are also stored here.

b) **Data Dictionary Cache:** The metadata of a database is called data dictionary. Almost any information you need to find about a database is stored in data dictionary. The data dictionary is accessed frequently. To speed up access, the contents are cached in shared pool in a special region named "data dictionary cache".

c) **Server Result Cache:** It is possible to cache results of a query in this region so that the next access to these results will be faster.

250: What is "Large Pool" in System Global Area?

Answer:

Large pool is an optional memory region inside System Global Area. It is used for operations where large size of memory needs to be allocated. For example, the large pool is used when taking backup with RMAN (Recovery Manager). The large pool also stores user global area (UGA) if you have shared server architecture. Additionally, the large pool is also used during parallel execution of SQL statements. The message buffers are kept in the large pool.

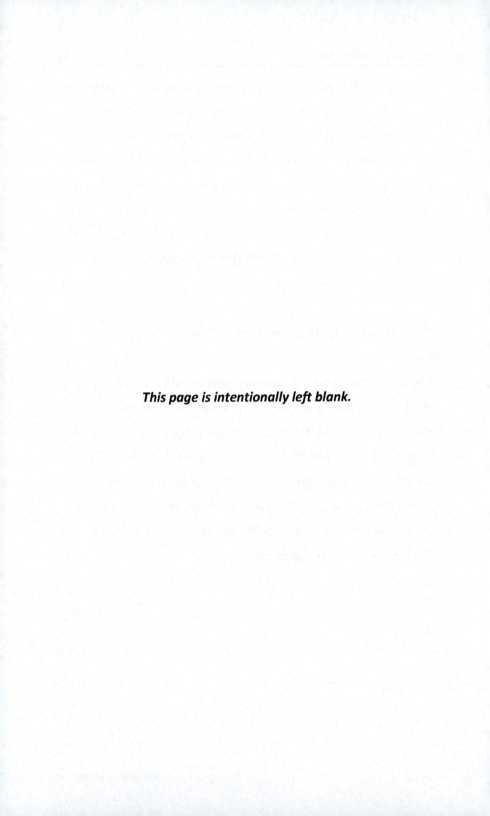
This page is intentionally left blank.

Chapter 18

Application and Networking Architecture

251: You have a client connection set with the database. With SQLDeveloper for example. While you are working, the database listener is killed by accident. Will you be able to commit your work after that moment?

Answer:

Yes. After the connection was set by the listener, the listener is no longer involved and the client has a direct connection with the database, allowing the work to be saved. The listener needs to be restarted for new connections to be established.

252: Explain the client-server architecture in Oracle Database environment.

Answer:

In client-server architecture, the data resides on the server. The processing is done on the server. Client is only used for presentation. The clients connect to server to send queries, the queries are processed by database server and the result is returned to the client. It is possible for client to be on the same computer with the server but the clients usually reside on a separate workstation. They make network connections to the database server. If client in installed on the server, they won't be a performance overhead for network transmission of results. Clients have the ability to connect to the database using IPC (Inter Process Communication).

253:What are the advantages of using client-server architecture?
Answer:
   a) The clients are independent from the server. You can place the clients anywhere you want as long as they have a network connection to the server.
   b) The clients can be optimized for representing data while server can be optimized for data processing. This provides separation of duty.
   c) The workstations don't have to be expensive hardware as their sole purpose is to present data.
   d) The shared data resides on only the database server. You don't have to copy the data to each client.

254: How does the distributed database architecture work?
Answer:
In a centralized architecture, the data resides on a single

hardware and all processing takes place on that server. In distributed database architecture, the data is distributed among several hardware. There will be multiple databases working at the same time. However the data will be distributed on these databases.

The processing tasks are also distributed. For example some part of a query might be executed on a database while the rest on a different database. This increases the total processing power of your applications.

255: What are the advantages of using distributed database architecture? Explain with an example.

Answer:

In distributed architecture, the total processing power of your environment is increased. You can divide the data and distribute processing tasks among the servers. Let's say you have a query which joins two tables. You can place one table in one database and place the other table on the second database. When you perform a select query, the read operations are performed separately by the databases where the tables reside. Another advantage is that all these distributed processing is done transparently. You can connect the databases with database links and execute the query at one database only. The query will be distributed to other databases implicitly.

256: Explain the multitier architecture in Oracle database environment.

Answer:

The most common multi-tier architecture is the 3 layer architecture. The first layer is the client computer and is the presentation layer. This is usually a workstation used by the end users.

At the second layer lies the application server. The clients make connection to the application servers. The application servers receive requests from clients and sends request to them.

At third layer, lies the database server. The application server makes connection to database server and send SQL queries to it. The database server receives the SQL requests, executes them and returns the result set to the application server. The clients don't make direct connection to database server.

257: What are the possible disadvantages of a multi-tier architecture?

Answer:

If you're using a multi-tier architecture, the clients do not directly connect to the database server. Instead they connect to the application server. The application server makes a connection on behalf of them. This makes tracking of end user activity difficult at database server.

For example, a web application might have thousands of users but at database layer they all share the same database user. You create a single database user for the application and all end user requests are executed by that single user.

258: What are the possible advantages of a multi-tier architecture?

Answer:

In early times in database technology, the architecture was mostly two layered. The clients used to make direct connections to database. For applications, where there was large number of end users, it was difficult to manage them because each end user had a database user.

Also you had to install Oracle client at each work station of the users because the users had to make direct connection. This made deployment process harder. You had to do installation and upgrade at later phases at each work station. However, in a multi-layered architecture, the Oracle client is only installed at application server.

259: How is a connection established in Oracle client/server architecture? What is the role of the listener?

Answer:

Oracle client software must be installed on a client workstation. The client application initiates the connection by calling the Oracle Call Interface (OCI) API. The client has to know the IP address of the listener, the port that the listener listens on and the service name of the database that it wants to connect to.

The listener is a process running on the database server. It listens on a specific port and accepts incoming requests. If a valid connection request comes, the listener creates a server process on the database server and redirects the client to that process.

260: What is service registration in Oracle NET architecture?

Answer:

When a client wants to make a connection to da database server, it connects to the listener processes first. The client has to know the IP address of the listener, the port number the listener process is listening. Once a connection is established, the client has to provide the service name he wants to connect and the username/password of the authenticating user. The listener process is responsible for creating a server process if the authentication is successful. Therefore the listener has to know which services are present and available on that server. Databases provide such information to listener processes. This is called service registration.

261: What is the difference between a static service registration and dynamic service registration?

Answer:

Listener processes are responsible for creating a server process and connecting the client processes to these server processes if the authentication succeeds. Therefore a listener process has to know which database services are available on a server. Informing the listener processes about the available services is called service registration. In static service registration, the service information is entered in listener.ora file manually. In dynamic service registration, the service information is periodically sent to the listener by the PMON process. Dynamic service registration is the recommended method by Oracle.

262: What is the advantage of using dynamic service registration over static registration?

Answer:

The information of available services are sent to listener processes so that the listener can create a proper server process and connect the client process to the server process. A database may have multiple services running on it. The services can be started or stopped while database is running. In a Real Application Cluster environment, a service can be relocated to other nodes in the cluster. The nature of service is dynamic. If you use static registration, you'll have to update listener.ora file each time the status of a service changes. This is not practical. However, while using dynamic service registration, the statuses of the services are automatically sent to listeners after a status update. This is more practical and reliable.

263: What is dedicated server architecture?

Answer:

A server process has to be created to execute requests coming from the clients. Listener processes are responsible for creating these processes and connect client processes to the relevant server process. Once a connection is established between the client process and server process, the client sends SQL queries to the server process. The server process executes these requests and returns the results to client process. After a session ends, the relevant server process is killed. During the life time of the session, that server process works exclusive to that client process. This is called dedicated server architecture.

264: Explain the Shared Server Architecture in Oracle Networking.

Answer:

A connection is established between a server process and a client process. The server process executes the incoming requests and sends back the results to client processes. In dedicated server architecture, the server process is exclusive to that client process. In shared server architecture, on server process can serve multiple clients requests. The dispatcher processes will accept the request from clients, they will deliver the request to shared server processes for executing and then they will get the results from shared server processes and send them back to the client process which has requested it.

265: What is the role of dispatcher processes in shared server architecture?

Answer:

In shared server architecture, the client request makes connection to a dispatcher process after it has contacted the listener process first. There will be multiple dispatcher processes on a database server. These dispatcher server processes accept the SQL queries coming from the clients and put it into "request queue". An available shared server process gets the request from the request queue, executes it and then places the result in "response queue". The relevant dispatcher process gets the results in the response queue and sends it back to the client which has requested it.

This page is intentionally left blank.

Chapter 19

Oracle Database Security

266: A user in your organization requested that you change the number of password attempts on his account from 3 to unlimited. How would you do this and why is this a bad idea security-wise?

Answer:

The profile for the user needs to be changed. The profile can be identified in the DBA_USERS table, PROFILE column. Then the FAILED_LOGIN_ATTEMPTS needs to be set to unlimited. However, this makes the account vulnerable to brute force password hacking attacks and should be avoided.

267: Explain what a privilege is and types of privileges.

Answer:

A privilege in Oracle database is the right to perform a specific action through SQL commands or queries. For example, once a user provides a valid username and password, he is authenticated to the database. This is allowed if the user has "CREATE SESSION" privileges. The privileges are categorized as and "OBJECT" privilege or "SYSTEM" privilege. "SYSTEM" privileges give database users the permission to carry out a specific action like "CREATE TABLE", "CREATE FUNCTION" etc. Object privileges give user the permission to perform specific actions on a database object. For instance, a user needs SELECT privilege on a table which he doesn't own to run SELECT queries on that table.

268: What are roles in Oracle database?
Answer:

A user will require certain privileges (either system privilege or object privileges) to perform certain operations in the database. For example, if a user wants to read the data inside a table, he needs SELECT privilege on that table. As a database administrator, you have to assign each privilege explicitly. Multiple users may need the same privileges. In this case, managing all those privileges may be a difficult task. To ease administration in such a situation, you first create a "role" and assign the required privileges to that role. Later, you assign that role to the users who require those privileges. This way, you don't have to assign privileges one by one to each user.

269: Explain the relationship between a database user and schema.

Answer:

A user in a database has a unique "username" inside the database and a password. A user can logon to database with his username and password. Once logged on, he can perform actions (executing SQL queries) that he is allowed to. A schema is a collection of objects owned by a user. The name of the schema equals to the username. User creates object, and that object is placed in the schema of that user. If the user has enough rights, he can also create objects which will be put in other user's schema.

270: What is use of "profiles" in Oracle?

Answer:

Each user in a database has a profile. A profile defines password management policy which that user has to comply with. It is also possible to limit the resources which that user can use. There is a default profile in database and every user is a member of that profile unless you explicitly assign the user to another profile. It is recommended to use Oracle "Resource Manager" to manage resource usage but profiles must be used for enforcing password management policies.

271: What are the password management attributes in user profiles?

Answer:

a) **FAILED_LOGIN_ATTEMPTS:** After how many invalid login attempts will the account be locked.

b) **PASSWORD_LIFE_TIME:** How long can a new password be used.

c) **PASSWORD_REUSE_TIME:** After how long can the user reuse the same password.

d) **PASSWORD_REUSE_MAX:** After how many password changes, can the user use the same password.

e) **PASSWORD_VERIFY_FUNCTION:** The Pl/SQL function which forces the complexity of the password.

f) **PASSWORD_LOCK_TIME:** How long will the account stay locked because of invalid login attempts?

g) **PASSWORD_GRACE_TIME:** How long will the user be warned about the expire time of the password before the account is locked.

272: Explain the Transparent Data Encryption option of Oracle Database.

Answer:

The "Transparent Data Encryption" (TDE) is an extra option in Oracle Enterprise Edition. It is used to encrypt individual columns or whole tablespace. A private key is created first and kept in Oracle Wallet. With the help of this key, you have the option of encrypting individual columns where sensitive information is kept. (for ex: Credit Card columns). It is also possible to encrypt a whole tablespace if everything on that tablespace is considered sensitive. It is called transparent encryption because all the encryption/decryption operations are handled automatically by Oracle at background. End users continue to execute SQL queries like they do with unencrypted tables.

273:Why would it be a good idea to use Transparent Data Encryption in Oracle Database?

Answer:

Oracle stores segment data as "open" on datafiles on disk. Open means it is readable. It is not encrypted. If an unauthorized person reaches those data files on disk, he can open the data file with a HEX editor and read sensitive data inside it. Oracle has its own format for keeping data, it is not much readable but if the attacker has knowledge of Oracle's format, he can locate the sensitive data inside a data file. To prevent sensitive data from such attacks, you can use TDE. With TDE, the sensitive data is kept as encrypted on disk. However, the data is decrypted when a user reads it, so the operation is transparent.

274: How does auditing work in Oracle Databases?

Answer:

For tracking access to sensitive data, you can use the auditing feature of Oracle. For using auditing, you first need to enable it. Enabling auditing is done by setting the "audit_trail" initialization parameter. This parameter enables the mechanism. After that, you need to specify which actions you want to audit. For example you can start auditing for DELETE operations for a specific table. Another setting you need to configure is where you want to store the audit trails. You can store the audit trails in a database table or in a regular file on disk outside the database.

275: What is the difference between standard auditing and fine-grained auditing?

Answer:

In the standard auditing mechanism, you can audit system privileges and object privileges. For object privileges, you can audit standard activities for the data manipulation like INSERT, DELETE, UPDATE and SELECT. These actions apply to the whole table. If you need to audit actions only on certain activities, or if you want to audit only for certain predicates (WHERE clauses) you need to use Fine Grained Auditing (FGA). For FGA, you define policies. The policies determine which columns, which actions and which predicates will be audited. Also, the audit trails from FGA go to a different table than the standard audit table.

Chapter 20

Maximum Availability Architecture

276: How would you protect your control files against hardware failures?

Answer:

The most usable way to protect control files is to multiplex them. When you multiplex control files, you place identical copies at separate hard disks. Oracle has the ability to keep identical copies for control files. Whatever written to one file is also written to other copies. This way, if one of the disks becomes faulty, you will have healthy copies on other disks. Another option will be to take a backup of the control file to a separate location (to another hard disk or to a tape drive) when you make a structural change in the database. You can restore the control files if the disks become unusable and you lose data.

277: How would you protect your online redo log files against hardware failures?

Answer:

The best way to protect online redolog files is to multiplex them. Each redo log group can have one or more members. Members are identical files inside a redo log group. Oracle writes to one group at a time. When writing to a redo log group, it writes to all members in that group. If you place the members on separate hardware, you'll have multiplexed your online redolog files. If one of the disks becomes faulty, Oracle can continue by using other members without affecting the end users. However, you'll receive messages in the alert log file about the relevant disk failure.

278: Explain the Real Application Cluster database architecture.

Answer:

In real application clusters, there will be multiple servers acting as a single database. The database will be single but there will be multiple instances running on separate hardware. The data is stored at a shared location usually in a Storage Area Network (SAN). Clients will connect to one of the nodes in the cluster. This provides load balancing.

Each server will have two network cards. One card is connected to the public network while other is connected to private network. The private network is used for inter-cluster communication. The public connection is used for connections with clients.

279: What are the advantages of using Real Application Clusters?

Answer:

There are two main advantages of using Real Application Clusters (RAC). One is high availability and other is processing power. The cluster is composed of two or more nodes. The nodes are separate servers each running their own database instance. If one of the servers goes down due to a hardware fault, the database still keeps on servicing clients from the other nodes.

Another advantage of using RAC is its ability to increase processing power with horizontal scaling. If you want to increase the total processing power of your database environment, you can add a new node to the cluster.

280: What would you do to provide fault tolerance to site failures?

Answer:

Most customers setup their database environment at one site. They take precautions to possible failures like multiplexing control files, redo log files etc. They also use RAC for high availability. They take regular backups to tape drivers. These cautions protect you from most of the possible failures you can meet. However, it is also possible that the site where you've installed your servers can also be harmed by natural disasters like fire, earthquakes, floods etc. In this case, your database service will be down. In worst case, you may lose data.

To protect your database against site failures is to use Oracle Data Guard. Oracle Data Guard is Oracle's stand by database solution. When you setup Oracle Data Guard, every change written to the primary database is also applied to the standby database. If the primary database environment goes that because of a failure, you can activate the standby database and start using it.

HR Questions

Review these typical interview questions and think about how you would answer them. Read the answers listed; you will find best possible answers along with strategies and suggestions.

1: Where do you find ideas?

Answer:

Ideas can come from all places, and an interviewer wants to see that your ideas are just as varied. Mention multiple places that you gain ideas from, or settings in which you find yourself brainstorming. Additionally, elaborate on how you record ideas or expand upon them later.

2: How do you achieve creativity in the workplace?

Answer:

It's important to show the interviewer that you're capable of being resourceful and innovative in the workplace, without stepping outside the lines of company values. Explain where ideas normally stem from for you (examples may include an exercise such as list-making or a mind map), and connect this to a particular task in your job that it would be helpful to be creative in.

3: How do you push others to create ideas?

Answer:

If you're in a supervisory position, this may be requiring employees to submit a particular number of ideas, or to complete regular idea-generating exercises, in order to work their creative muscles. However, you can also push others around you to create ideas simply by creating more of your own. Additionally, discuss with the interviewer the importance of questioning people as a way to inspire ideas and change.

4: Describe your creativity.

Answer:

Try to keep this answer within the professional realm, but if you have an impressive background in something creative outside of your employment history, don't be afraid to include it in your answer also. The best answers about creativity will relate problem-solving skills, goal-setting, and finding innovative ways to tackle a project or make a sale in the workplace. However, passions outside of the office are great, too (so long as they don't cut into your work time or mental space).

5: Would you rather receive more authority or more responsibility at work?

Answer:

There are pros and cons to each of these options, and your interviewer will be more interested to see that you can provide a critical answer to the question. Receiving more authority may mean greater decision-making power and may be great for those with outstanding leadership skills, while greater responsibility may be a growth opportunity for those looking to advance steadily throughout their careers.

6: What do you do when someone in a group isn't contributing their fair share?

Answer:

This is a particularly important question if you're interviewing for a position in a supervisory role – explain the ways in which you would identify the problem, and how you would go about pulling aside the individual to discuss their contributions. It's important to understand the process of creating a dialogue, so that you can communicate your expectations clearly to the individual, give them a chance to respond, and to make clear what needs to change. After this, create an action plan with the group member to ensure their contributions are on par with others in the group.

7: Tell me about a time when you made a decision that was outside of your authority.

Answer:

While an answer to this question may portray you as being decisive and confident, it could also identify you to an employer as a potential problem employee. Instead, it may be best to slightly refocus the question into an example of a time that you took on additional responsibilities, and thus had to make decisions that were outside of your normal authority (but which had been granted to you in the specific instance). Discuss how the weight of the decision affected your decision-making process, and the outcomes of the situation.

8: Are you comfortable going to supervisors with disputes?

Answer:

If a problem arises, employers want to know that you will handle it in a timely and appropriate manner. Emphasize that you've rarely had disputes with supervisors in the past, but if a situation were to arise, you feel perfectly comfortable in discussing it with the person in question in order to find a resolution that is satisfactory to both parties.

9: If you had been in charge at your last job, what would you have done differently?

Answer:

No matter how many ideas you have about how things could run better, or opinions on the management at your previous job, remain positive when answering this question. It's okay to show thoughtful reflection on how something could be handled in order to increase efficiency or improve sales, but be sure to keep all of your suggestions focused on making things better, rather than talking about ways to eliminate waste or negativity.

10: Do you believe employers should praise or reward employees for a job well done?

Answer:

Recognition is always great after completing a difficult job, but there are many employers who may ask this question as a way to infer as to whether or not you'll be a high-maintenance worker. While you may appreciate rewards or praise, it's important to convey to the interviewer that you don't require accolades to be confident that you've done your job well. If you are interviewing for a supervisory position where you would be the one praising other employees, highlight the importance of praise in boosting team morale.

11: What do you believe is the most important quality a leader can have?

Answer:

There are many important skills for a leader to have in any business, and the most important component of this question is that you explain why the quality you choose to highlight is important. Try to choose a quality such as communication skills, or an ability to inspire people, and relate it to a specific instance in which you displayed the quality among a team of people.

12: Tell me about a time when an unforeseen problem arose. How did you handle it?

Answer:

It's important that you are resourceful, and level-headed under pressure. An interviewer wants to see that you handle problems systematically, and that you can deal with change in an orderly process. Outline the situation clearly, including all solutions and results of the process you implemented.

13: Can you give me an example of a time when you were able to improve X objective at your previous job?

Answer:

It's important here to focus on an improvement you made that created tangible results for your company. Increasing efficiency is certainly a very important element in business, but employers are also looking for concrete results such as increased sales or cut expenses. Explain your process thoroughly, offering specific numbers and evidence wherever possible, particularly in outlining the results.

14: Tell me about a time when a supervisor did not provide specific enough direction on a project.

Answer:

While many employers want their employees to follow very specific guidelines without much decision-making power, it's important also to be able to pick up a project with vague direction and to perform self-sufficiently. Give examples of necessary questions that you asked, and specify how you determined whether a question was something you needed to ask of a supervisor or whether it was something you could determine on your own.

15: Tell me about a time when you were in charge of leading a project.

Answer:

Lead the interviewer through the process of the project, just as you would have with any of your team members. Explain the goal of the project, the necessary steps, and how you delegated tasks to your team. Include the results, and what you learned as a result of the leadership opportunity.

16: Tell me about a suggestion you made to a former employer that was later implemented.
Answer:
Employers want to see that you're interested in improving your company and doing your part – offer a specific example of something you did to create a positive change in your previous job. Explain how you thought of the idea, how your supervisors received it, and what other employees thought was the idea was put into place.

17: Tell me about a time when you thought of a way something in the workplace could be done more efficiently.
Answer:
Focus on the positive aspects of your idea. It's important not to portray your old company or boss negatively; so don't elaborate on how inefficient a particular system was. Rather, explain a situation in which you saw an opportunity to increase productivity or to streamline a process, and explain in a general step-by-step how you implemented a better system.

18: Is there a difference between leading and managing people – which is your greater strength?

Answer:

There is a difference – leaders are often great idea people, passionate, charismatic, and with the ability to organize and inspire others, while managers are those who ensure a system runs, facilitate its operations, make authoritative decisions, and who take great responsibility for all aspects from overall success to the finest decisions. Consider which of these is most applicable to the position, and explain how you fit into this role, offering concrete examples of your past experience.

19: Do you function better in a leadership role, or as a worker on a team?

Answer:

It is important to consider what qualities the interviewer is looking for in your position, and to express how you embody this role. If you're a leader, highlight your great ideas, drive and passion, and ability to incite others around you to action. If you work great in teams, focus on your dedication to the task at hand, your cooperation and communication skills, and your ability to keep things running smoothly.

20: Tell me about a time when you discovered something in the workplace that was disrupting your (or others) productivity – what did you do about it?

Answer:

Try to not focus on negative aspects of your previous job too much, but instead choose an instance in which you found a positive, and quick, solution to increase productivity. Focus on the way you noticed the opportunity, how you presented a solution to your supervisor, and then how the change was implemented (most importantly, talk about how you led the change initiative). This is a great opportunity for you to display your problem-solving skills, as well as your resourceful nature and leadership skills.

21: How do you perform in a job with clearly-defined objectives and goals?

Answer:

It is important to consider the position when answering this question – clearly, it is best if you can excel in a job with clearly-defined objectives and goals (particularly if you're in an entry level or sales position). However, if you're applying for a position with a leadership role or creative aspect to it, be sure to focus on the ways that you additionally enjoy the challenges of developing and implementing your own ideas.

22: How do you perform in a job where you have great decision-making power?

Answer:

The interviewer wants to know that, if hired, you won't be the type of employee who needs constant supervision or who asks for advice, authority, or feedback every step of the way. Explain that you work well in a decisive, productive environment, and that you look forward to taking initiative in your position.

23: If you saw another employee doing something dishonest or unethical, what would you do?

Answer:

In the case of witnessing another employee doing something dishonest, it is always best to act in accordance with company policies for such a situation – and if you don't know what this company's specific policies are, feel free to simply state that you would handle it according to the policy and by reporting it to the appropriate persons in charge. If you are aware of the company's policies (such as if you are seeking a promotion within your own company), it is best to specifically outline your actions according to the policy.

24: Tell me about a time when you learned something on your own that later helped in your professional life.

Answer:

This question is important because it allows the interviewer to gain insight into your dedication to learning and advancement. Choose an example solely from your personal life, and provide a brief anecdote ending in the lesson you learned. Then, explain in a clear and thorough manner how this lesson has translated into a usable skill or practice in your position.

25: Tell me about a time when you developed a project idea at work.

Answer:

Choose a project idea that you developed that was typical of projects you might complete in the new position. Outline where your idea came from, the type of research you did to ensure its success and relevancy, steps that were included in the project, and the end results. Offer specific before and after statistics, to show its success.

26: Tell me about a time when you took a risk on a project.
Answer:

Whether the risk involved something as complex as taking on a major project with limited resources or time, or simply volunteering for a task that was outside your field of experience, show that you are willing to stretch out of your comfort zone and to try new things. Offer specific examples of why something you did was risky, and explain what you learned in the process – or how this prepared you for a job objective you later faced in your career.

27: What would you tell someone who was looking to get into this field?
Answer:

This question allows you to be the expert – and will show the interviewer that you have the knowledge and experience to go along with any training and education on your resume. Offer your knowledge as advice of unexpected things that someone entering the field may encounter, and be sure to end with positive advice such as the passion or dedication to the work that is required to truly succeed.

28: How would you handle a negative coworker?
Answer:

Everyone has to deal with negative coworkers – and the single best way to do so is to remain positive. You may try to build a relationship with the coworker or relate to them in some way, but even if your efforts are met with a cold shoulder, you must retain your positive attitude. Above all, stress that you would never allow a coworker's negativity to impact your own work or productivity.

29: What would you do if you witnessed a coworker surfing the web, reading a book, etc, wasting company time?
Answer:

The interviewer will want to see that you realize how detrimental it is for employees to waste company time, and that it is not something you take lightly. Explain the way you would adhere to company policy, whether that includes talking to the coworker yourself, reporting the behavior straight to a supervisor, or talking to someone in HR.

30: How do you handle competition among yourself and other employees?
Answer:

Healthy competition can be a great thing, and it is best to stay focused on the positive aspects of this here. Don't bring up conflict among yourself and other coworkers, and instead focus on the motivation to keep up with the great work of others, and the ways in which coworkers may be a great support network in helping to push you to new successes.

31: When is it okay to socialize with coworkers?

Answer:

This question has two extreme answers (all the time, or never), and your interviewer, in most cases, will want to see that you fall somewhere in the middle. It's important to establish solid relationships with your coworkers, but never at the expense of getting work done. Ideally, relationship-building can happen with exercises of teamwork and special projects, as well as in the break room.

32: Tell me about a time when a major change was made at your last job, and how you handled it.

Answer:

Provide a set-up for the situation including the old system, what the change was, how it was implemented, and the results of the change, and include how you felt about each step of the way. Be sure that your initial thoughts on the old system are neutral, and that your excitement level grows with each step of the new change, as an interviewer will be pleased to see your adaptability.

33: When delegating tasks, how do you choose which tasks go to which team members?

Answer:

The interviewer is looking to gain insight into your thought process with this question, so be sure to offer thorough reasoning behind your choice. Explain that you delegate tasks based on each individual's personal strengths, or that you look at how many other projects each person is working on at the time, in order to create the best fit possible.

34: Tell me about a time when you had to stand up for something you believed strongly about to coworkers or a supervisor.

Answer:

While it may be difficult to explain a situation of conflict to an interviewer, this is a great opportunity to display your passions and convictions, and your dedication to your beliefs. Explain not just the situation to the interviewer, but also elaborate on why it was so important to you to stand up for the issue, and how your coworker or supervisor responded to you afterward – were they more respectful? Unreceptive? Open-minded? Apologetic?

35: Tell me about a time when you helped someone finish their work, even though it wasn't "your job."

Answer:

Though you may be frustrated when required to pick up

someone else's slack, it's important that you remain positive about lending a hand. The interviewer will be looking to see if you're a team player, and by helping someone else finish a task that he or she couldn't manage alone, you show both your willingness to help the team succeed, and your own competence.

36: What are the challenges of working on a team? How do you handle this?

Answer:

There are many obvious challenges to working on a team, such as handling different perspectives, navigating individual schedules, or accommodating difficult workers. It's best to focus on one challenge, such as individual team members missing deadlines or failing to keep commitments, and then offer a solution that clearly addresses the problem. For example, you could organize weekly status meetings for your team to discuss progress, or assign shorter deadlines in order to keep the long-term deadline on schedule.

37: Do you value diversity in the workplace?

Answer:

Diversity is important in the workplace in order to foster an environment that is accepting, equalizing, and full of different perspectives and backgrounds. Be sure to show your awareness of these issues, and stress the importance of learning from others' experiences.

38: How would you handle a situation in which a coworker was not accepting of someone else's diversity?

Answer:

Explain that it is important to adhere to company policies regarding diversity, and that you would talk to the relevant supervisors or management team. When it is appropriate, it could also be best to talk to the coworker in question about the benefits of alternate perspectives – if you can handle the situation yourself, it's best not to bring resolvable issues to management.

39: Are you rewarded more from working on a team, or accomplishing a task on your own?

Answer:

It's best to show a balance between these two aspects – your employer wants to see that you're comfortable working on your own, and that you can complete tasks efficiently and well without assistance. However, it's also important for your employer to see that you can be a team player, and that you understand the value that multiple perspectives and efforts can bring to a project.

40: Tell me about a time when you didn't meet a deadline.

Answer:

Ideally, this hasn't happened – but if it has, make sure you use a minor example to illustrate the situation, emphasize how long ago it happened, and be sure that you did as much as you could to ensure that the deadline was met. Additionally, be sure to include what you learned about managing time better or prioritizing tasks in order to meet all future deadlines.

41: How do you eliminate distractions while working?
Answer:

With the increase of technology and the ease of communication, new distractions arise every day. Your interviewer will want to see that you are still able to focus on work, and that your productivity has not been affected, by an example showing a routine you employ in order to stay on task.

42: Tell me about a time when you worked in a position with a weekly or monthly quota to meet. How often were you successful?
Answer:

Your numbers will speak for themselves, and you must answer this question honestly. If you were regularly met your quotas, be sure to highlight this in a confident manner and don't be shy in pointing out your strengths in this area. If your statistics are less than stellar, try to point out trends in which they increased toward the end of your employment, and show reflection as to ways you can improve in the future.

43: Tell me about a time when you met a tough deadline, and how you were able to complete it.

Answer:

Explain how you were able to prioritize tasks, or to delegate portions of an assignment to other team members, in order to deal with a tough deadline. It may be beneficial to specify why the deadline was tough – make sure it's clear that it was not a result of procrastination on your part. Finally, explain how you were able to successfully meet the deadline, and what it took to get there in the end.

44: How do you stay organized when you have multiple projects on your plate?

Answer:

The interviewer will be looking to see that you can manage your time and work well – and being able to handle multiple projects at once, and still giving each the attention it deserves, is a great mark of a worker's competence and efficiency. Go through a typical process of goal-setting and prioritizing, and explain the steps of these to the interviewer, so he or she can see how well you manage time.

45: How much time during your work day do you spend on "auto-pilot?"

Answer:

While you may wonder if the employer is looking to see how efficient you are with this question (for example, so good at your job that you don't have to think about it), but in almost every case, the employer wants to see that you're constantly thinking, analyzing, and processing what's going on in the workplace. Even if things are running smoothly, there's usually an opportunity somewhere to make things more efficient or to increase sales or productivity. Stress your dedication to ongoing development, and convey that being on "auto-pilot" is not conducive to that type of success.

46: How do you handle deadlines?
Answer:
The most important part of handling tough deadlines is to prioritize tasks and set goals for completion, as well as to delegate or eliminate unnecessary work. Lead the interviewer through a general scenario, and display your competency through your ability to organize and set priorities, and most importantly, remain calm.

47: Tell me about your personal problem-solving process.
Answer:
Your personal problem-solving process should include outlining the problem, coming up with possible ways to fix the problem, and setting a clear action plan that leads to resolution. Keep your answer brief and organized, and explain the steps in a concise, calm manner that shows you are level-headed even under stress.

48: What sort of things at work can make you stressed?

Answer:

As it's best to stay away from negatives, keep this answer brief and simple. While answering that nothing at work makes you stressed will not be very believable to the interviewer, keep your answer to one generic principle such as when members of a team don't keep their commitments, and then focus on a solution you generally employ to tackle that stress, such as having weekly status meetings or intermittent deadlines along the course of a project.

49: What do you look like when you are stressed about something? How do you solve it?

Answer:

This is a trick question – your interviewer wants to hear that you don't look any different when you're stressed, and that you don't allow negative emotions to interfere with your productivity. As far as how you solve your stress, it's best if you have a simple solution mastered, such as simply taking deep breaths and counting to 10 to bring yourself back to the task at hand.

50: Can you multi-task?

Answer:

Some people can, and some people can't. The most important part of multi-tasking is to keep a clear head at all times about what needs to be done, and what priority each task falls under.

Explain how you evaluate tasks to determine priority, and how you manage your time in order to ensure that all are completed efficiently.

51: How many hours per week do you work?
Answer:

Many people get tricked by this question, thinking that answering more hours is better – however, this may cause an employer to wonder why you have to work so many hours in order to get the work done that other people can do in a shorter amount of time. Give a fair estimate of hours that it should take you to complete a job, and explain that you are also willing to work extra whenever needed.

52: How many times per day do you check your email?
Answer:

While an employer wants to see that you are plugged into modern technology, it is also important that the number of times you check your email per day is relatively low – perhaps two to three times per day (dependent on the specific field you're in). Checking email is often a great distraction in the workplace, and while it is important to remain connected, much correspondence can simply be handled together in the morning and afternoon.

53: Tell me about a time when you worked additional hours to finish a project.

Answer:

It's important for your employer to see that you are dedicated to your work, and willing to put in extra hours when required or when a job calls for it. However, be careful when explaining why you were called to work additional hours – for instance, did you have to stay late because you set goals poorly earlier in the process? Or on a more positive note, were you working additional hours because a client requested for a deadline to be moved up on short notice? Stress your competence and willingness to give 110% every time.

54: Tell me about a time when your performance exceeded the duties and requirements of your job.

Answer:

If you're a great candidate for the position, this should be an easy question to answer – choose a time when you truly went above and beyond the call of duty, and put in additional work or voluntarily took on new responsibilities. Remain humble, and express gratitude for the learning opportunity, as well as confidence in your ability to give a repeat performance.

55: What is your driving attitude about work?

Answer:

There are many possible good answers to this question, and the interviewer primarily wants to see that you have a great passion for the job and that you will remain motivated in your career if hired. Some specific driving forces behind your success may include hard work, opportunity, growth potential, or success.

56: Do you take work home with you?

Answer:

It is important to first clarify that you are always willing to take work home when necessary, but you want to emphasize as well that it has not been an issue for you in the past. Highlight skills such as time management, goal-setting, and multi-tasking, which can all ensure that work is completed at work.

57: Describe a typical work day to me.

Answer:

There are several important components in your typical work day, and an interviewer may derive meaning from any or all of them, as well as from your ability to systematically lead him or her through the day. Start at the beginning of your day and proceed chronologically, making sure to emphasize steady productivity, time for review, goal-setting, and prioritizing, as well as some additional time to account for unexpected things that may arise.

58: Tell me about a time when you went out of your way at your previous job.

Answer:

Here it is best to use a specific example of the situation that required you to go out of your way, what your specific position would have required that you did, and how you went above that. Use concrete details, and be sure to include the results, as well as reflection on what you learned in the process.

59: Are you open to receiving feedback and criticisms on your job performance, and adjusting as necessary?

Answer:

This question has a pretty clear answer – yes – but you'll need to display knowledge as to why this is important. Receiving feedback and criticism is one thing, but the most important part of that process is to then implement it into your daily work. Keep a good attitude, and express that you always appreciate constructive feedback.

60: What inspires you?

Answer:

You may find inspiration in nature, reading success stories, or mastering a difficult task, but it's important that your inspiration is positively-based and that you're able to listen and tune into it when it appears. Keep this answer generally based in the professional world, but where applicable, it may stretch a bit into creative exercises in your personal life that, in turn, help you in achieving career objectives.

61: How do you inspire others?

Answer:

This may be a difficult question, as it is often hard to discern the effects of inspiration in others. Instead of offering a specific example of a time when you inspired someone, focus on general principles such as leading by example that you employ in your professional life. If possible, relate this to a quality that someone who inspired you possessed, and discuss the way you have modified or modeled it in your own work.

62: How do you make decisions?
Answer:

This is a great opportunity for you to wow your interviewer with your decisiveness, confidence, and organizational skills. Make sure that you outline a process for decision-making, and that you stress the importance of weighing your options, as well as in trusting intuition. If you answer this question skillfully and with ease, your interviewer will trust in your capability as a worker.

63: What are the most difficult decisions for you to make?
Answer:

Explain your relationship to decision-making, and a general synopsis of the process you take in making choices. If there is a particular type of decision that you often struggle with, such as those that involve other people, make sure to explain why that type of decision is tough for you, and how you are currently engaged in improving your skills.

64: When making a tough decision, how do you gather information?

Answer:

If you're making a tough choice, it's best to gather information from as many sources as possible. Lead the interviewer through your process of taking information from people in different areas, starting first with advice from experts in your field, feedback from coworkers or other clients, and by looking analytically at your own past experiences.

65: Tell me about a decision you made that did not turn out well.

Answer:

Honesty and transparency are great values that your interviewer will appreciate – outline the choice you made, why you made it, the results of your poor decision – and finally (and most importantly!) what you learned from the decision. Give the interviewer reason to trust that you wouldn't make a decision like that again in the future.

66: Are you able to make decisions quickly?

Answer:

You may be able to make decisions quickly, but be sure to communicate your skill in making sound, thorough decisions as well. Discuss the importance of making a decision quickly, and how you do so, as well as the necessity for each decision to first be well-informed.

67: Describe a time when you communicated a difficult or complicated idea to a coworker.

Answer:

Start by explaining the idea briefly to the interviewer, and then give an overview of why it was necessary to break it down further to the coworker. Finally, explain the idea in succinct steps, so the interviewer can see your communication abilities and skill in simplification.

68: What situations do you find it difficult to communicate in?

Answer:

Even great communicators will often find particular situations that are more difficult to communicate effectively in, so don't be afraid to answer this question honestly. Be sure to explain why the particular situation you name is difficult for you, and try to choose an uncommon answer such as language barrier or in time of hardship, rather than a situation such as speaking to someone of higher authority.

69: What are the key components of good communication?

Answer:

Some of the components of good communication include an environment that is free from distractions, feedback from the listener, and revision or clarification from the speaker when necessary. Refer to basic communication models where necessary, and offer to go through a role-play sample with the interviewer in order to show your skills.

70: Tell me about a time when you solved a problem through communication?

Answer:

Solving problems through communication is key in the business world, so choose a specific situation from your previous job in which you navigated a messy situation by communicating effectively through the conflict. Explain the basis of the situation, as well as the communication steps you took, and end with a discussion of why communicating through the problem was so important to its resolution.

71: Tell me about a time when you had a dispute with another employee. How did you resolve the situation?

Answer:

Make sure to use a specific instance, and explain step-by-step the scenario, what you did to handle it, and how it was finally resolved. The middle step, how you handled the dispute, is clearly the most definitive – describe the types of communication you used, and how you used compromise to reach a decision. Conflict resolution is an important skill for any employee to have, and is one that interviewers will search for to determine both how likely you are to be involved in disputes, and how likely they are to be forced to become involved in the dispute if one arises.

72: Do you build relationships quickly with people, or take more time to get to know them?

Answer:

Either of these options can display good qualities, so determine which style is more applicable to you. Emphasize the steps you take in relationship-building over the particular style, and summarize briefly why this works best for you.

73: Describe a time when you had to work through office politics to solve a problem.

Answer:

Try to focus on the positives in this question, so that you can use the situation to your advantage. Don't portray your previous employer negatively, and instead use a minimal instance (such as paperwork or a single individual), to highlight how you worked through a specific instance resourcefully. Give examples of communication skills or problem-solving you used in order to achieve a resolution.

74: Tell me about a time when you persuaded others to take on a difficult task?

Answer:

This question is an opportunity to highlight both your leadership and communication skills. While the specific situation itself is important to offer as background, focus on how you were able to persuade the others, and what tactics worked the best.

75: Tell me about a time when you successfully persuaded a group to accept your proposal.

Answer:

This question is designed to determine your resourcefulness and your communication skills. Explain the ways in which you took into account different perspectives within the group, and created a presentation that would be appealing and convincing to all members. Additionally, you can pump up the proposal itself by offering details about it that show how well-executed it was.

76: Tell me about a time when you had a problem with another person, that, in hindsight, you wished you had handled differently.

Answer:

The key to this question is to show your capabilities of reflection and your learning process. Explain the situation, how you handled it at the time, what the outcome of the situation was, and finally, how you would handle it now. Most importantly, tell the interviewer why you would handle it differently now – did your previous solution create stress on the relationship with the other person, or do you wish that you had stood up more for what you wanted? While you shouldn't elaborate on how poorly you handled the situation before, the most important thing is to show that you've grown and reached a deeper level of understanding as a result of the conflict.

77: Tell me about a time when you negotiated a conflict between other employees.

Answer:

An especially important question for those interviewing for a supervisory role – begin with a specific situation, and explain how you communicated effectively to each individual. For example, did you introduce a compromise? Did you make an executive decision? Or, did you perform as a mediator and encourage the employees to reach a conclusion on their own?

Index

Oracle Database Administration Interview Questions

Basic Administration

1: You as a DBA just gathered the statistics on schema A. Schema A has 1500 tables. You want to know the name of the table with the highest number of records without running a count on each. How do you do this?

2: List four possible ways (direct or indirect) to execute an SQL query against an Oracle Database.

3: What is SQL*Plus? How can one acquire it and what kind of operations can be performed with it?

4: A user is logged on to a Linux server as root where Oracle database is running. The Oracle is installed at "/u01/app/oracle/product/11.2.0.4/dbhome" and the name of the SID is "ORCL". The user wants to connect to the database locally using operating system authentication with SYSDBA privileges. Show the command that the user has to execute.

5: In our organization, we're using an Oracle database whose version is 11.2.0.4. Explain what each digit shows.

6: You're at a client's office and you are expected to solve a problem in their database. The client is not sure about their database version and you want to find out the version of their existing database. Describe three different methods you can use to find the version of database software.

7: Your client said that he forgot the password for "SYSTEM" user of his database and he no longer could connect. How would you recover this admin password?

8: What is a password file and why is it needed?

9: You want to find out how many users are defined in the password file and what privileges those user have. How would you accomplish this?

10: What would be the main responsibilities of an Oracle DBA in an organization?

11: How does an Oracle DBA role differ from an Oracle Developer role in an organization? Are there any similarities between these too?

Creating and Configuring an Oracle Database

12: How do you choose the DB character set, and how is it changed after the database is created?

13: There are 10 identical servers and you want to install Oracle Database on each of them. What would you use to automate the installation process?

14: You want to create a response file to speed up the installation of databases. How would you prepare a response file?

15: When creating a database with SQL script, what would you specify in the script?

16: What makes up an Oracle Instance?

17: What constitutes an Oracle Database?

Database States and Database Operations

18: You are informed by monitoring that database PROD2 is down. When you issue startup the database enters mount but fails to proceed to the next stage. What file allows the database to enter mount mode, and where do you expect to be problems to move past that?

19: Which tools can you use to start up an Oracle database?

20: During startup of a database, at which order does Oracle software search a parameter file?

21: At what stages does an instance pass while starting up?

22: You want to do maintenance on your database but during the maintenance period, you don't want any user to be able to connect to the database. How would you accomplish this?

23: Your database is open. You don't want to interrupt currently connected users but you want to temporarily disable further logons. What would you do to achieve this and how would you revert the database back to normal state after that?

24: What are the types of shutdown modes of an Oracle database?

25: The data files of your database reside on a storage system. You want to take a snapshot of the storage so that you can use it backup purposes. You also want to ensure that no data is written to data files while the snapshot is being taken. Is it possible to accomplish this while the database is open?

26: What kind of information can be given while creating a sequence?

Oracle Background Processes

27: Oracle starts many background processes. Which one will cause the instance to crash if it is killed? Which infrastructure event is this similar to?

28: You look in the server and find there are 5 processes starting with P and followed by numbers, P000, P001 up to P004. What are these processes?

29: The LOG_ARCHIVE_MAX_PROCESSES parameter controls the maximum number of processes responsible for which task? What are the names of these processes in the OS? How many are spawned at startup?

30: You want your database to start automatically, after a reboot of the server.

How would you do that?

31: Which components of your database environment can be protected by an "Oracle Restart" configuration?

32: Explain the difference between "shared server" architecture and "dedicated server" architecture.

33: Explain how "shared server" architecture works.

34: What are the instance parameters that are used for configuring shared server architecture?

35: Explain how the "Database Writer" process works.

36: Explain what role "Log Writer" background process plays in an instance.

37: What is a checkpoint in an Oracle Database?

38: How does an instance recovery occur in an instance?

39: How does archiving of online redo log files happen in an instance?

40: What is an "External Procedure Call"?

41: Where can it be useful to use an "External Procedure Call"?

42: What are the types of processes in an Oracle environment?

43: What is the duty of "Process Monitor" (PMON) process in an Oracle database instance?

44: What are the two Manageability Monitor background processes and what do they do?

Patches and Upgrades

45: Suppose that an 11.2.0.2 database supports several applications, each with its own schema. Can you upgrade one of those schemas to 11.2.0.4 keeping the rest on the older version, to support policy requirements?

46: What are the names of the two scripts that are executed as a part of the manual upgrade procedure?

47: How do you apply a patch to a database? Where do you get the file, what are the generic steps and what is the name of the command to perform the actual task?

Database External Utilities

48: How do you use datapump to import a dumpfile from a database on server A to a different database on server B?

49: You have a CSV file that you wish to load in a table. Which oracle utility can you use for this?

50: What utility do you use to change the DBID? Why would you do this?

Sessions and Processes

51: If a database has reached its maximum number of allowed processes, how can you increase this value?

52: A user contacts you saying that an update is taking too long. You check and find there is a session blocking the table with a wait of "SQL*Net message from client". Is this a problem?

53: You run top (or topas in AIX or process explorer in windows) and find that the process ID 10020 is consuming CPU for the last hour. How can you find the session SID of the corresponding session in the database?

54: How does Oracle execute scheduler jobs and which background processes take part in this?

55: You have an application server named "SPARC12" in your organization. You want to find users who are currently connected to from that server. How would you do that?

56: In your organization, the application developers use SQL Developer program to connect to database. You want to find out the database username of the developers who are currently connected with SQL Developer. Write an SQL query for this.

57: You know that one of the employees in the company is connected to the database. His username in the active directory of the company is "joe.black" and the domain name of your company is "grey". Write a query to find the name of the computer that this user is connected from and port of the physical connection.

58: Explain what the below query is retrieving.
sql> SELECT command,status FROM v$session WHERE username='SCOTT';

59: You want to disconnect all the users of you CRM application. You know that the database username of that CRM application is CRM2014. How would you disconnect all users of that application while the rest of the database remains fully operational?

60: The server administrator has says that he has detected an operating system process which consumes large memory and high CPU. If the server administrator gives you the process id, can you find which session this process belongs?

Schemas and Schema Objects

61: In 11gr2, to use the UTL_FILE package what kind of database objects do you need to create to allow access to the filesystem?

62: You have 2 indexes on a table: on column A and a compound index on column A,B. Does a query on column B choose any of these indexes column B use?

63: You as user A, need to access table LOGS in user B's schema. User B grants you select on the table, but when you run SELECT COUNT(1) FROM LOGS you receive a table doesn't exist error. Why?

64: What is the relationship between a schema and a user in an Oracle database?

65: List the object types that a schema can contain in an Oracle database.

66: How are schema objects stored logically? What is the relationship between these logical structures?

67: How is a "view" stored in an Oracle database and how does it differ than the way a "table" is stored?

68: How are the schema objects stored physically? What is the relationship between these physical structures?

69: What is schema object dependency? How does this mechanism work?

70: What are the administrative schemas in an Oracle Database?

71: What is a sample schema? What are the sample schemas that can be installed?

72: What are the three types of tables according to the way the rows are organized?

73: What is the difference between a "permanent table" and a "temporary table"?

74: What is the minimum information required to create a table?

75: You have reached a table of a web application. What objects can be expected to be found on this table?

76: What kind of constraints can you define on a column?

77: Explain a physical table in an Oracle Database in terms of Logical Data Modeling.

78: How does the character set affect a database?

79: Explain the difference between "byte semantics" and "character semantics" in a table.

80: Explain the "varchar2" data type and how it differs from a "char" data type.

81: What are the NVARCHAR2 and NCHAR data types?

82: If you want to store the time zone data along with the date, which data types can you use in a column?

83: What is a rowid? What does a rowid show?

84: Explain the "rowid" and "rownum" pseudo columns.

85: Explain why indexes are used so commonly and how they work.

86: Under what circumstances would it be a good idea to use indexes?

87: What is the difference between an usable index and an invisible index?

88: What are reverse key indexes and why are they used?

89: What is descending index and why would it be a good idea to use it?

90: What is a function-based index and where should it be used?

91: When should you choose bitmap indexes over B*tree indexes?

92: What is a view as a schema object?

93: What is the force option used for when creating a view?

94: Explain why it would be a good idea to use a view?

95: What is a materialized view and how does it differ from a regular view?

96: What is the difference between a "complete refresh" and a "fast refresh" in materialized views?

97: How are the sequences incremented in Oracle?

98: How would you select the current value of a sequence and how does this method behave for concurrent separate sessions?

99: Why would you want to use the CACHE feature of sequences?

100: You have an "employees" table in your application. You want to assign an employee id which will uniquely identify each employee. You want the employee id to increment by one and you don't want any gap between two employee ids. The developer thinks that it would be improper to use a sequence to accomplish task. Explain why it will be a bad idea to use a sequence here.

101: Explain the "synonym" schema object?

102: What is the difference between a private synonym and a public synonym?

103: Explain where it would be a good idea to use synonyms and give examples for them.

Data Integrity

104: What are the techniques at a database level to guarantee data integrity to avoid application issues?

105: What is a "NOT NULL" constraint and where is it used?

106: What is a "unique constraint" and why would you need that?

107: What is a primary key? Where is it used?

108: What is the difference between a primary key constraint and a unique key constraint?

109: What is a "natural key" and a "surrogate key"? What is the difference between these two?

110: What is a foreign key constraint?

111: What are the options of cascade if a record in the parent table is deleted or updated?

112: What can be done to improve performance and usability of foreign key constraints?

113: What is a check constraint?

114: What is the difference between an "ENABLE VALIDATE" and "ENABLE NOVALIDATE" constraint?

115: Explain the difference between a "deferrable" constraint and a "non-deferrable" constraint.

Data Dictionary and Dynamic Performance Views

116: As a DBA you want to know which objects on schema B does user A have privileges. Where do you go for this information?

117: A user reports that he has a query running for more than one hour. How do you find his session and what is the value of the TYPE column for his session?

118: Explain what a "base table" and a "view" means in a data dictionary.

119: What are the three prefixes that are seen in the data dictionary views?

120: What is the use of the "DUAL" table in the data dictionary?

121: What are dynamic performance views in a database?

SQL

122: What parts can be found in a regular SELECT statement?

123: Explain the DDL statements in SQL.

124: What is DML in SQL?

125: Explain the type of "joins" that can be found in an SQL statement.

126: What are the three types of outer joins?

127: What is an implicit SELECT query?

128: What are the Transaction Control Statements?

129: Explain the Session Control Statements.

130: Explain the most widely used access paths that the optimizer performs.

131: What are the four types of optimizer statistics?

132: What is an "Optimizer Hint"?

133: What are the three types of checks that are performed during SQL parsing phase?

Programming

134: Explain how a client-side program interacts with an Oracle database.

135: What is the difference between a thin driver and a thick driver?

136: Explain server-side programming?

137: What is Oracle Client Software and why is it needed?

138: Why would a stored PL/SQL program perform better than an anonymous PL/SQL block?

139: In which schema objects can you store the PL/SQL code you've written?

140: List out three advantages that you can gain by using a PL/SQL package.

141: What constructs can be found in a PL/SQL Code?

142: Why does working with batch collections perform better than working on a single record at a time?

143: What events can fire a trigger in a database?

144: Why would you use triggers in a database?

145: What is the difference between a "row trigger" and a "statement trigger"?

146: Explain the times when a trigger can be configured to run.

147: When would it be a good idea to use "before" triggers? Explain with an example.

148: When would it be a good idea to use "after" triggers? Explain with an example.

Data Concurrency and Consistency

149: User A is running a long uncommitted transaction with several DML statements on table Z. User B queries table Z 60 minutes after user A started and gets the ORA-01555 error. What does this mean?

150: What is read consistency in an Oracle Database?

151: What is a dirty read? Explain with an example.

152: From the isolation levels, explain how "read committed" transactions behave?

153: From the isolation levels, explain how "serializable" transactions behave?

154: Explain how readers and writers interact with each other according to the row locking mechanism in Oracle.

155: What is the difference between an exclusive lock and a shared lock?

156: Tell us about the life time of an exclusive row lock and give an example.

157: How does a deadlock occur? Explain with an example.

158: Explain how Oracle manages row locks?

Transactions

159: User A is running a long uncommitted transaction with several DML statements on table Z. User B queries table Z and doesn't see the changed data. After 30 minutes he gets the ORA-01555 error. What happened?

160: What is a transaction?

161: Give an example of a business process where using a transaction would be necessary.

162: List all the possibilities a transaction can end.

163: What is the difference between the statement -level atomicity and transaction-level atomicity?

164: What can be advantage of naming a transaction?

165: What is an "active" transaction and what is the effect of an active transaction on the database structures?

166: What happens when a commit occurs for a transaction either explicitly or implicitly?

167: What happens when a rollback occurs for a transaction either explicitly

or implicitly?
168: What is an autonomous transaction?
169: What is a distributed transaction?

Storage Structures
170: You have one datafile in a mount point /opt. Due to application data growth, the datafile has maxed out the available space. You want to reduce the size of the datafile. The application team, deletes a huge table of historical data. Was this enough?
171: What are the physical structures of an Oracle Database?
172: Where can you store a database file? What are the alternatives?
173: What are the advantages of using ASM (Automatic Storage Management) over a regular file system?
174: What is the relationship between an ASM disk and an ASM disk group?
175: Explain the relationship between an ASM extent, ASM Allocation Unit, ASM file and ASM Disk Group.
176: What is an ASM instance? How does it work?
177: Explain how data is organized physically inside database?
178: Explain how data is organized logically inside database?
179: At what points does a temporary data file differ from a permanent data file?
180: When are temporary tablespaces used?
181: What are the statuses of data files?
182: What kind of information is stored in a control file?
183: Explain the control file importance for a database and how it can be protected.
184: How do online redo log files work?
185: Explain what happens when a user updates a record in the database?
186: How can we protect our online redo log files?
187: What is archived log file and why are they used?
188: Explain the relationship between a database data block and an operating system block.
189: How can ROWID be used to locate a row?
190: Explain what "Row Chaining" and "Row Migration" means.
191: Why do we need undo segments in an Oracle database?
192: What is High Water Mark (HWM)?
193: What are the default tablespaces found in an Oracle database?
194: What is undo retention in an Oracle database?

Oracle Instance Architecture
195: If you have a Data Guard configuration with one primary and one

standby, and the standby for network reasons lags beyond the available archives on the primary, how do you fix the issue?

196: You have a 3 node Oracle RAC. A user creates 3 different connections from 3 different clients (for example: sqlplus, sqldeveloper and excel) on the same machine. Do all these connections go to the same node?

197: Can you have ASM configured with RAC? What are the benefits of having ASM configured?

198: What are the differences between single instance architecture and RAC architecture?

199: At what stages does an instance pass respectively while starting up ?

200: With what privileges can you connect to an instance?

201: How does Oracle start an instance?

202: What does mounting a database mean and what operations can be performed on the database while it is in a mount state?

203: How is a database opened after the mount stage?

204: At what stages does an open Oracle instance pass until it is shut down?

205: Explain what happens during a checkpoint and why is it needed?

206: What happens during instance recovery?

207: When does an instance recovery occur? How do you start it?

208: What kind of messages can be found in an alert log file?

209: What are the basic memory structures found in an Oracle instance?

210: What are the options of managing Oracle instance memory?

211: What are the parts of Program Global Area (PGA)?

212: What is the role of database buffer cache?

213: What are the states of buffers in database buffer cache?

214: When are the dirty blocks written to disk?

215: What is "current mode get" and "consistent read get"?

216: What is the use of redo log buffer inside System Global Area (SGA)?

217: Explain the structure of the Shared Pool inside SGA?

218: What is the difference between a "soft parse" and a "hard parse"?

219: What would you do to minimize the hard parses?

220: What is Large Pool and where is it used?

221: Explain the "Software Code Area" memory areas.

222: What are the main types of processes you can find in an Oracle environment?

223: What is the difference between "dedicated server architecture" and "shared server architecture"?

224: What is the duty of the SMON background process?

225: When does the log writer process write redo records from the buffer to disk?

226: Why is it a bad idea at performance perspective to commit too frequently?

227: What is the role of "checkpoint" process in an instance?

228: What are the most common three types of checkpoints?

229: When do thread checkpoints occur?

230: What are the two types of instance parameter s?

231: What is the difference between a text based parameter file and server parameter file?

232: Explain the directory structure of Automatic Diagnostic Repository.

233: What are the main directories and files found in Automatic Diagnostic Repository (ADR) for an RDBMS?

234: What kind of messages is stored in "alert.log" file?

Oracle Database Memory Structures

235: When a new query is issued on the database an execution plan is generated. Is this before or after parsing and in which structure of the database are the execution plans stored?

236: What are the characteristics of Shared Global Area (SGA)?

237: What are the characteristics of Program Global Area (PGA)?

238: What are the options of managing the memory of an instance?

239: What are the two different options when using Automatic Memory Management?

240: What is User Global Area (UGA) and how it behaves differently in Shared Server Architecture and Dedicated Server Architecture?

241: Describe what Private SQL Area is.

242: Describe what SQL Work Areas are.

243: Why is a mechanism like "database buffer cache" needed in an Oracle Instance?

244: What are the three types of data block buffer states?

245: What are the two buffer mode gets?

246: What is the difference between a physical read and logical read?

247: What are the three types of buffer pools in database buffer cache?

248: What is redolog buffer used for?

249: What are the sub-components of shared pool? Explain them briefly.

250: What is "Large Pool" in System Global Area?

Application and Networking Architecture

251: You have a client connection set with the database. With SQLDeveloper for example. While you are working, the database listener is killed by accident. Will you be able to commit your work after that moment?

252: Explain the client-server architecture in Oracle Database environment.

253: What are the advantages of using client-server architecture?

254: How does the distributed database architecture work?
255: What are the advantages of using distributed database architecture? Explain with an example.
256: Explain the multitier architecture in Oracle database environment.
257: What are the possible disadvantages of a multi-tier architecture?
258: What are the possible advantages of a multi-tier architecture?
259: How is a connection established in Oracle client/server architecture? What is the role of the listener?
260: What is service registration in Oracle NET architecture?
261: What is the difference between a static service registration and dynamic service registration?
262: What is the advantage of using dynamic service registration over static registration?
263: What is dedicated server architecture?
264: Explain the Shared Server Architecture in Oracle Networking.
265: What is the role of dispatcher processes in shared server architecture?

Oracle Database Security

266: A user in your organization requested that you change the number of password attempts on his account from 3 to unlimited. How would you do this and why is this a bad idea security-wise?
267: Explain what a privilege is and types of privileges.
268: What are roles in Oracle database?
269: Explain the relationship between a database user and schema.
270: What is use of "profiles" in Oracle?
271: What are the password management attributes in user profiles?
272: Explain the Transparent Data Encryption option of Oracle Database.
273: Why would it be a good idea to use Transparent Data Encryption in Oracle Database?
274: How does auditing work in Oracle Databases?
275: What is the difference between standard auditing and fine-grained auditing?

Maximum Availability Architecture

276: How would you protect your control files against hardware failures?
277: How would you protect your online redo log files against hardware failures?
278: Explain the Real Application Cluster database architecture?
279: What are the advantages of using Real Application Clusters?
280: What would you do to provide fault tolerance to site failures?

HR Questions

1: Where do you find ideas?

2: How do you achieve creativity in the workplace?

3: How do you push others to create ideas?

4: Describe your creativity.

5: Would you rather receive more authority or more responsibility at work?

6: What do you do when someone in a group isn't contributing their fair share?

7: Tell me about a time when you made a decision that was outside of your authority.

8: Are you comfortable going to supervisors with disputes?

9: If you had been in charge at your last job, what would you have done differently?

10: Do you believe employers should praise or reward employees for a job well done?

11: What do you believe is the most important quality a leader can have?

12: Tell me about a time when an unforeseen problem arose. How did you handle it?

13: Can you give me an example of a time when you were able to improve X objective at your previous job?

14: Tell me about a time when a supervisor did not provide specific enough direction on a project.

15: Tell me about a time when you were in charge of leading a project.

16: Tell me about a suggestion you made to a former employer that was later implemented.

17: Tell me about a time when you thought of a way something in the workplace could be done more efficiently.

18: Is there a difference between leading and managing people – which is your greater strength?

19: Do you function better in a leadership role, or as a worker on a team?

20: Tell me about a time when you discovered something in the workplace that was disrupting your (or others) productivity – what did you do about it?

21: How do you perform in a job with clearly-defined objectives and goals?

22: How do you perform in a job where you have great decision-making power?

23: If you saw another employee doing something dishonest or unethical, what would you do?

24: Tell me about a time when you learned something on your own that later helped in your professional life.

25: Tell me about a time when you developed a project idea at work.

26: Tell me about a time when you took a risk on a project.

27: What would you tell someone who was looking to get

28: How would you handle a negative coworker?

29: What would you do if you witnessed a coworker surfing the web, reading a book, etc, wasting company time?

30: How do you handle competition among yourself and other employees?

31: When is it okay to socialize with coworkers?

32: Tell me about a time when a major change was made at your last job, and how you handled it.

33: When delegating tasks, how do you choose which tasks go to which team members?

34: Tell me about a time when you had to stand up for something you believed strongly about to coworkers or a supervisor

35: Tell me about a time when you helped someone finish their work, even though it wasn't "your job."

36: What are the challenges of working on a team? How do you handle this?

37: Do you value diversity in the workplace?

38: How would you handle a situation in which a coworker was not accepting of someone else's diversity?

39: Are you rewarded more from working on a team, or accomplishing a task on your own?

40: Tell me about a time when you didn't meet a deadline.

41: How do you eliminate distractions while working?

42: Tell me about a time when you worked in a position with a weekly or monthly quota to meet. How often

43: Tell me about a time when you met a tough deadline, and how you were able to complete it.

44: How do you stay organized when you have multiple

45: How much time during your work day do you spend on "auto-pilot?"

46: How do you handle deadlines?

47: Tell me about your personal problem-solving process.

48: What sort of things at work can make you stressed?

49: What do you look like when you are stressed about something? How do you solve it?

50: Can you multi-task?

55: What is your driving attitude about work?

56: Do you take work home with you?

57: Describe a typical work day to me.

58: Tell me about a time when you went out of your way at your previous job.

59: Are you open to receiving feedback and criticisms on your job performance, and adjusting as necessary?

Some of the following titles might also be handy:

1. .NET Interview Questions You'll Most Likely Be Asked
2. 200 Interview Questions You'll Most Likely Be Asked
3. Access VBA Programming Interview Questions You'll Most Likely Be Asked
4. Adobe ColdFusion Interview Questions You'll Most Likely Be Asked
5. Advanced Excel Interview Questions You'll Most Likely Be Asked
6. Advanced JAVA Interview Questions You'll Most Likely Be Asked
7. Advanced SAS Interview Questions You'll Most Likely Be Asked
8. AJAX Interview Questions You'll Most Likely Be Asked
9. Algorithms Interview Questions You'll Most Likely Be Asked
10. Android Development Interview Questions You'll Most Likely Be Asked
11. Ant & Maven Interview Questions You'll Most Likely Be Asked
12. Apache Web Server Interview Questions You'll Most Likely Be Asked
13. Artificial Intelligence Interview Questions You'll Most Likely Be Asked
14. ASP.NET Interview Questions You'll Most Likely Be Asked
15. Automated Software Testing Interview Questions You'll Most Likely Be Asked
16. Base SAS Interview Questions You'll Most Likely Be Asked
17. BEA WebLogic Server Interview Questions You'll Most Likely Be Asked
18. C & C++ Interview Questions You'll Most Likely Be Asked
19. C# Interview Questions You'll Most Likely Be Asked
20. C++ Internals Interview Questions You'll Most Likely Be Asked
21. CCNA Interview Questions You'll Most Likely Be Asked
22. Cloud Computing Interview Questions You'll Most Likely Be Asked
23. Computer Architecture Interview Questions You'll Most Likely Be Asked
24. Computer Networks Interview Questions You'll Most Likely Be Asked
25. Core JAVA Interview Questions You'll Most Likely Be Asked
26. Data Structures & Algorithms Interview Questions You'll Most Likely Be Asked
27. Data WareHousing Interview Questions You'll Most Likely Be Asked
28. EJB 3.0 Interview Questions You'll Most Likely Be Asked
29. Entity Framework Interview Questions You'll Most Likely Be Asked
30. Fedora & RHEL Interview Questions You'll Most Likely Be Asked
31. GNU Development Interview Questions You'll Most Likely Be Asked
32. Hibernate, Spring & Struts Interview Questions You'll Most Likely Be Asked
33. HTML, XHTML and CSS Interview Questions You'll Most Likely Be Asked
34. HTML5 Interview Questions You'll Most Likely Be Asked
35. IBM WebSphere Application Server Interview Questions You'll Most Likely Be Asked
36. iOS SDK Interview Questions You'll Most Likely Be Asked
37. Java / J2EE Design Patterns Interview Questions You'll Most Likely Be Asked
38. Java / J2EE Interview Questions You'll Most Likely Be Asked
39. Java Messaging Service Interview Questions You'll Most Likely Be Asked
40. JavaScript Interview Questions You'll Most Likely Be Asked
41. JavaServer Faces Interview Questions You'll Most Likely Be Asked
42. JDBC Interview Questions You'll Most Likely Be Asked
43. jQuery Interview Questions You'll Most Likely Be Asked
44. JSP-Servlet Interview Questions You'll Most Likely Be Asked
45. JUnit Interview Questions You'll Most Likely Be Asked
46. Linux Commands Interview Questions You'll Most Likely Be Asked
47. Linux Interview Questions You'll Most Likely Be Asked
48. Linux System Administrator Interview Questions You'll Most Likely Be Asked
49. Mac OS X Lion Interview Questions You'll Most Likely Be Asked
50. Mac OS X Snow Leopard Interview Questions You'll Most Likely Be Asked

51. Microsoft Access Interview Questions You'll Most Likely Be Asked
52. Microsoft Excel Interview Questions You'll Most Likely Be Asked
53. Microsoft Powerpoint Interview Questions You'll Most Likely Be Asked
54. Microsoft Word Interview Questions You'll Most Likely Be Asked
55. MySQL Interview Questions You'll Most Likely Be Asked
56. NetSuite Interview Questions You'll Most Likely Be Asked
57. Networking Interview Questions You'll Most Likely Be Asked
58. OOPS Interview Questions You'll Most Likely Be Asked
59. Operating Systems Interview Questions You'll Most Likely Be Asked
60. Oracle Database Administration Interview Questions You'll Most Likely Be Asked
61. Oracle E-Business Suite Interview Questions You'll Most Likely Be Asked
62. ORACLE PL/SQL Interview Questions You'll Most Likely Be Asked
63. Perl Interview Questions You'll Most Likely Be Asked
64. PHP Interview Questions You'll Most Likely Be Asked
65. PMP Interview Questions You'll Most Likely Be Asked
66. Python Interview Questions You'll Most Likely Be Asked
67. RESTful JAVA Web Services Interview Questions You'll Most Likely Be Asked
68. Ruby Interview Questions You'll Most Likely Be Asked
69. Ruby on Rails Interview Questions You'll Most Likely Be Asked
70. SAP ABAP Interview Questions You'll Most Likely Be Asked
71. SAS STAT and Programming Interview Questions You'll Most Likely Be Asked
72. Selenium Testing Tools Interview Questions You'll Most Likely Be Asked
73. Silverlight Interview Questions You'll Most Likely Be Asked
74. Software Repositories Interview Questions You'll Most Likely Be Asked
75. Software Testing Interview Questions You'll Most Likely Be Asked
76. SQL Server Interview Questions You'll Most Likely Be Asked
77. Tomcat Interview Questions You'll Most Likely Be Asked
78. UML Interview Questions You'll Most Likely Be Asked
79. Unix Interview Questions You'll Most Likely Be Asked
80. UNIX Shell Programming Interview Questions You'll Most Likely Be Asked
81. VB.NET Interview Questions You'll Most Likely Be Asked
82. XLXP, XSLT, XPATH, XFORMS & XQuery Interview Questions You'll Most Likely Be Asked
83. XML Interview Questions You'll Most Likely Be Asked

For complete list visit

www.vibrantpublishers.com

CPSIA information can be obtained
at www.ICGtesting.com
Printed in the USA
LVOW13s1524130617
537963LV00010B/639/P